Paradise Is a State of Mind

ALEXIA EDEN

Copyright © 2023 Alexia Eden

All rights reserved.
No part of this book may be reproduced by any mechanical, photographic, or electronic process, or in the form of a phonographic recording; nor may it be stored in a retrieval system, transmitted, or otherwise be copied for public or private use – other than for 'fair use' as brief quotations embodied in articles and reviews – without prior written permission of the publisher.

The author of this book does not dispense medical advice or prescribe the use of any technique as a form of treatment for physical, emotional, or medical problems without the advice of a physician, either directly or indirectly. The intent of the author is only to offer information of a general nature to help you in your quest for well-being. In the event you use any of the information in this book for yourself, which is your constitutional right, the author assumes no responsibility for your actions.

Author photograph: Enrico Bruschi
Editor: Ashten Luna Evans
Cover design | photograph: Alexia Eden
Interior design: Alexia Eden

ISBN: 9798335018623

If you Believe in Yourself,
Anything is Possible

CONTENTS

Introduction		vii
1	What You Give Out, You Get Back	Pg 1
2	The Giver	Pg 11
3	Abundance Is the Love of the Universe	Pg 23
4	The Star of the Show	Pg 35
5	When It Is All Finished, You Will Discover It Was Never Random.	Pg 49
6	A Cat That Always Lands on Their Feet	Pg 59
7	If You Believe In Yourself, Anything Is Possible	Pg 81
8	Goals, Ambitions and Dreams	Pg 101
9	Soulmates	Pg 113
10	Sacral Beauty	Pg 133
11	Ease, Fun, Bliss, Magic & The Flow	Pg 147
12	Paradise, Love, Gratitude and Heaven on Earth	Pg 163

Epilogue	Pg 175
Acknowledgements	Pg 181
Soul Journey	Pg 187
Recommended Reading	Pg 197

-INTRODUCTION-

*P*aradise Is a State of Mind is a collection of positive new thought ideas and affirmations designed to saturate your mind with the energies of positivity, joy and gratitude! To me, love, joy and gratitude are the highest-vibrational feelings one can experience, and the keys to Paradise. Paradise is a state of mind; a bliss mindset where you see the beauty, joy and wonder in everything – including the so-called 'bad' experiences. When you fixate your mind upon the beauty, joy and good in your world, your mind and being vibrate Paradise – and Paradise manifests all around you. Your world becomes a living Heaven on Earth.

This book is based upon my own experiences of what I have learnt about life so far and how it works. Our journey of life is different for everyone, but I hope that this book helps at least one person who has had (or

-INTRODUCTION-

would like to have) similar experiences! I find that when we read books or hear from people who have similar journeys to ours, it helps to solidify our experiences and to feel more connected with one another, to Life and with everything!

The universe is made of Love, and when we give out love, positivity, joy and gratitude, we receive it back! Not only do we get back what we give out, but when we emit positive energies such as love, optimism, joy, passion, creation, etc., they come back tenfold. As we are appreciating and giving out the very fabric of the universe itself, our efforts are returned in abundance. Life, i.e. Love, loves to create more of itself!

The Universe expands Love and positivity exponentially and in tandem, your own capacity and power to create and to *be* Love is endless! You have tremendous, infinite power to Love, and the Universe responds to *you*. You are the Source of love, joy, positivity, power, fulfilment, self-belief, creation, wonder and awe in your world. Everything comes from you and is at one with you. You are the Power, Love, Oneness and Paradise.

We were created by Love and made one with Love.

Paradise Is a State of Mind

Love – the Power that creates us – is still here! It is ever-present. The Power that created us is with us at all times, even when we can't see it. A Power much bigger than us and yet one with us is constantly guiding us, watching over us, loving us, and leading us to our Higher Good and greatest potential; expanding and becoming more of who we truly *are*.

There is only one Power in the universe, and we are one with it! You are the Universe and you are the Power that created you; you are one. This means that the only thing 'out there' that can ever seemingly harm you is just your own negative thoughts! There is no 'other' or 'out there'. Nobody, no person, other power or force has any power over you. The Power of our own minds and oneness with Source is a trillion times more powerful than any 'out there'. The Power we have from oneness with Source and ourselves is so powerful, it isn't even measurable. It is infinite.

What we focus on, grows! We have been gifted the power of our own minds and focus. Just as we can unwittingly create negativity in our lives, we can also just as equally and even more powerfully create Positivity and Paradise! When we train our minds and beings to focus on positivity, goodness and Love, we

-INTRODUCTION-

begin to see it grow and then flourish in our lives! If we are overly affixed on the negative, then generally we grow weeds and scraggy plants in our garden of life. However, as we fix our minds on positivity, gratitude, and all the feel-good energies, we instead create the most gorgeous, beautiful, fragrant flowers, rich colourful array of flora and fauna, and the tallest, most lush, verdant, magnificent trees! The garden of your mind and your life will become a living Paradise: Eden. You reap what you sow. Sow seeds of positivity, gratitude and joy, and this is the Eden created.

Creating Paradise.~

Often, the simplest changes we implement turn out to be the most powerful, life-transforming and profound.

Starting small, with the simplest change or two, soon adds up and compounds to exponential growth and returns over time! Like planting the tiniest fruit tree seed or flower bulb in your garden, this humble seed or bulb soon grows up to produce the most glorious, grand gorgeous blooms and rich abundant fruits with time! Just like the seeds of flowers and fruits in nature,

Paradise Is a State of Mind

our love and positivity yield phenomenal returns.

The one thing I have found instrumental in creating Heaven on Earth is gratitude. Gratitude unlocks all doors. Gratitude creates beauty where there was only ugly thorns and wilderness, oases in the middle of desert and reveals the brightest stars amidst the darkest night sky! Gratitude *is* Heaven on Earth. It is the ultimate experience of Paradise and Oneness because when you are truly grateful, in that moment you feel you have everything you could ever want or need. Gratitude is fullness, completion and wholeness. The outer world is a mirror that reflects the inner and so as you feel gratitude, fullness and wholeness on the inside, Heaven on Earth and completion manifests externally.

As we improve our mindsets to think positively, we create a more solid external positive reality. The outer world is always a mirror; a reflection of our own inner thoughts, beliefs and vibrations. In order to create lasting change in ourselves and our lives, we begin on the initial adventure of training our minds. Practically speaking, we attune and train our minds with repetition to think and *be* positive. As we think positive, we send positive energy out into the universe.

-INTRODUCTION-

In order to train our mind, we must treat it like any other muscle. The mind is a muscle and like all muscles it takes regular training, persistence, patience and recovery to strengthen, develop and thrive!

Practising new, small daily positive habits will add up over time to create enormous and beneficial notable change. A powerful practice to begin with is a simple gratitude practice where we list 3-5 good things that happened during our day. I believe the best time to do this is at the end of your day just before you go to sleep, when your subconscious mind is most receptive to the new! Over time, you continually reinforce with your list to your subconscious mind that good things happen, that life is a good place and that you are lucky and fortunate and blessed! Your mind begins to reshape and see yourself as 'lucky' or 'loved by the Universe!' Your faith and trust in Life will grow, and your belief that good things are normal for you and that Life is on your side will become stronger and stronger! Gratitude and positive energy multiplies. Over time, your efforts will add up, compound and overflow. Your mind will become such a strong, serendipitous and positive magnet for love, positive energies, blessings and fortune that your life will look miraculous from the outside! But inside, you will know that you have

Paradise Is a State of Mind

created it.

~.Paradise Affirmations

In addition to gratitude, positive affirmations are the second practice I have found most instrumental in creating a life of Heaven on Earth. Positive affirmations are creation statements that describe the life you are forming right now. When you say or write positive affirmations, you are visualizing your future and saturating in the energies of what it feels like to have already achieved your goals! As you align with the feeling of realizing your goals through using positive affirmations, the practised consistency of that alignment eventually creates the conditions that allow their realization.

I have included positive affirmations at the end of almost every chapter of this book, in order to reinforce the themes and ideas of that chapter! The chapter themes include positivity, receiving, abundance, success, destiny, luck, challenges, optimism and self-belief, goals and dreams, soulmates, beauty and confidence, releasing anxiety and choosing Trust, and

-INTRODUCTION-

finally creating Paradise – Heaven on Earth! These affirmations are designed to attune your vibration so that you are vibrating closer to Heaven on Earth! The more frequently you practise and reside at Heaven on Earth frequencies, the more second nature, natural and normal they will become and the faster, more powerfully and permanently you will be pulled into the magnetic and irresistible allure of Paradise!

Practise the affirmations that you're drawn to on that day at that time. Your subconscious mind will draw you to the right affirmations you need for that day; just trust and follow your intuition! It is normal to be drawn to different affirmations on different days as we are constantly in motion and flux. Really, what we are truly doing underneath is practising and strengthening our own vibrational alignment to Paradise, via regularly practising the energies that make us feel good! The more we feel good, or even paradisiacal, the more we become and emit that magnetic energy into the universe, drawing back like-vibrational circumstances, people and events that help us to feel more of the same! It becomes an endless, self-reinforcing cycle.

Paradise Is a State of Mind

~.Final Thoughts.~

Please note that throughout this book I use varying capitalization of certain words, like Love and Life. In these cases, I use the capitalization to indicate these words as proper nouns. Love, as referred to in this book, is another term for the Power that created the universe, or the vibrational field of Love. Life is also a proper noun used to describe the Higher Power, or the undercurrent directing the universe. Self with a capital 'S' generally refers to the Higher Self, which everyone has. Generally, these capitalizations refer to something of Divinity.

The Higher Power referred to in this book has multiple names: Universe, God, Source, Creator, Divine Intelligence, Angels, etc. Throughout the book I use the names that I use personally, however if another name feels right to you, please feel free to just replace what I wrote with your own personal way of addressing the Higher Power. The most important thing is that it is harmonizing to *you*.

Finally, it is fine to have bad days or days where we don't always do it perfectly! As humans, we don't stay positive 100% of the time and our lives are constantly in

-INTRODUCTION-

ebb and flow. It is part of the growth and progress process to 'slip up' or have setbacks. However, as long as we keep going and put our efforts in, it will always be more than enough! The Universe helps us where we can't help ourselves. The more you keep going, the more you'll notice miracles and magic appearing to pick you back up again whenever you fall out of Flow. It is truly amazing!

Fix your mind on everything that is going right in your life and think thoughts of love, joy and gratitude, and you will attune more and more to the reality that Life is on your side and deeply loves you. You create a life of your wildest dreams and beyond. As you emit Paradise, you receive Paradise back. Life supports you whatever you put out, so tuning in to the wavelength that Life is working in your favour always, and tirelessly conspiring for your utter fulfilment and happiness, will allow you to see the evidence appear in your life and world – magnifying it a hundredfold!

Enjoy your journey to Paradise!

1.

-WHAT YOU GIVE OUT, YOU GET BACK-

This chapter includes positive affirmations for thinking positive and changing your mindset to one of Positivity. What we give out, we get back! Think positive thoughts, feel positive emotions, vibrate positive energy and good will come back to you! Do it as often as possible.

Positive thoughts are much stronger than negative ones. They have more vibrational Power and gravitas, therefore if you think positive thoughts some of the time, the Positive energy will spiral upwards and you will begin to attract more and more good back to you. Put out the energy of love, joy and gratitude and love, joy and gratitude will come back to you ten times over! Positive energy and these high-vibrational emotions are so strong that they bring back more of their likeness ten times over. Love is generous and giving.

It doesn't matter if you have negative thoughts, as they are weak, and as long as you are doing your best to fill

-WHAT YOU GIVE OUT, YOU GET BACK-

your mind with positivity, the Positivity will eventually take over, dominate and crowd out all the negativity from your mind. Positivity also makes you much more resilient to negative thoughts – and easier to bounce back from anything undesired during the day.

Keep practising! Like attracts like; the more you practise thinking positive thoughts, the more they will begin to take over and fill your consciousness and it becomes easier and easier! **Positivity will become your default reality.**

Positivity really is a choice – your choice. Choice is power. You have the choice and the power to be as positive as you want – to create a life of unlimited good as much as you want! You can choose to be positive over being negative. It just starts with a simple shift; *choosing* to be positive. When you change the way you look at things, the things you look at change. Positivity transforms the world around you; and yourself. Your mind becomes paradisiacal to live in, and you will manifest a world around you of Paradise, reflecting back these heavenly thoughts. Most importantly, being positive feels *good*! There is no better feeling than living in the Paradise of your own positive thoughts. Choose to begin being positive today, and you will soon see it is a far easier and more joyful way to live!

Paradise Is a State of Mind

~•POSITIVITY AFFIRMATIONS•~

- I think positive, helpful, uplifting thoughts!

- My mind is full of Positivity!

- My mind is full of Positivity and Light.

- I am the happiest person I know!

- My mind is full of Love, joy and Paradise.

- My mind is full of Love, optimism and joy.

- My being is full of love, passion, joy and gratitude!

- I see love everywhere, in every person, place and thing I meet.

- My mind is full of Love.

- My heart is beautiful and my mind is beautiful. I am kind and wise. I love what I see in me.

- I am my own best friend.

-WHAT YOU GIVE OUT, YOU GET BACK-

- I am my own cheerleader.

- I believe in myself.

- I am amazing.

- I can do anything.

- I love myself!

- I have the most empowering, helpful, positive inner game.

- My self-talk is empowering and uplifting.

- I love what I see in me.

- I am the best.

- I am my number one admirer, or one of them.

- I love and appreciate myself.

- I admire myself!

- I love and believe in myself.

- I am always there for myself.

- I am a winner!

Paradise Is a State of Mind

- I radiate positive energy and self-belief.

- I radiate positivity, self-belief and love.

- I uplift everyone I meet.

- I am exciting and positive.

- I am fun to be around.

- People love me and I love people. I am always at home in the universe.

- I only ever see the good in life! I love and trust Life. I know that Life is benevolent and loving.

- I love and trust *myself*.

- I always make the right decisions for me.

- I have flawless intuition.

- I respect and admire myself! I am amazing.

- I love and enjoy myself. Life is amazing.

- I always see the good in people. I attract loving, helpful, friendly positive people in my world.

-WHAT YOU GIVE OUT, YOU GET BACK-

- I think positive, loving, helpful, encouraging thoughts about others.

- I only ever think the most loving, positive, helpful, encouraging uplifting thoughts about myself.

- I am Love and Positivity.

- I radiate Positive energy.

- Positivity and Love fill my life.

- Passion and excitement fill my life.

- Positivity, love and laughter fill my life.

- I always see the good in life.

- I am so blessed and so lucky!

- I am grateful for everything. I love life!

- I love dwelling on how fortunate, lucky and blessed I am.

- My mind is a living Paradise. My world is a creation of Heaven on Earth.

- Every day I wake up appreciating my blessings.

Paradise Is a State of Mind

- I deserve every wonderful thing I have created for myself. I am worthy and deserving of the very best and I love life!

- I am magical and Fire.

- I am grateful and positive.

- I am lucky and resilient.

- I turn every so-called 'setback' that happens to me into an opportunity.

- The Universe loves me and deeply approves of everything I do.

- I really am the best. I love myself.

- I love my mind, my heart, my body, my soul and my life! I am so glad to be me. I appreciate myself.

- I love every setback, every lesson, every event and every happy experience that has made me who I am.

- Everything happens **for** me. The Universe has a plan that is always for my Highest Good. I am always being guided.

-WHAT YOU GIVE OUT, YOU GET BACK-

- I am always riding the wings of Fortune.

- I am very important to the Universe and Life works with me tirelessly to fulfil my dreams.

- I radiate luck, resilience and Positive energy.

- I radiate good luck, opportunity and outrageous fortune!

- I radiate Love, Positivity, gratitude and blessings!

- I am exciting and uplifting to be around.

- I am brave and a risk-taker!

- I am adventurous, fearless and passionate.

- I have the courage to pursue my dreams.

- I always follow myself. I am my best Leader.

- Everybody loves me and I love myself.

- I see Life through the eyes of love, gratitude and connection.

- I see the world through eyes of opportunity, adventure and luck.

Paradise Is a State of Mind

- I am daring and courageous.

- I am fearless.

- I love life! Life is exciting and unpredictable. I love stepping out into the unknown.

- There is untold good in my future.

- I live a life of Paradise. I give out Paradise, and I get back Paradise 10x over.

- Everything always works out in my favour.

- Even when I lose, I win.

- I am Love, Magic, Fire and Bliss.

- I am a whirlwind of Love, Positivity, Luck and Magic.

- I radiate pure, loving, powerful, radiant Positive energy.

- What you give out, you get back. I give out goodness, and only goodness comes back to me.

- I am living in the Paradise of my own creation.

-WHAT YOU GIVE OUT, YOU GET BACK-

- Life is on my side. I love Life.

2.

-THE GIVER-

A ffirm your luck, blessings and the good that is coming to you, and that is exactly what will materialize in your world and more!

The Universe is abundant, generous, limitless, and a Giver, and you are the centre of its attention and affections. We are all beloved children of the Universe. You do not have to do anything in order to receive from the Universe – you are worthy and deserving already just because you *are*. You are so loved by the infinite, loving, awe-inspiring Universe that that makes you automatically worthy! A limitless, benevolent, infinite supernatural Power loves you so much that it created you and then made you aware of your own power to create. That is how much the Universe loves you.

The Universe is infinite, inexhaustible and creative and it loves to lavish you with abundance, good, love, joy and blessings. The Universe wants to impress you, surprise you, sweep you off your feet and awe you! It

-THE GIVER-

wants to give you even more and better than what you want. That's why your heart always knows what makes you happiest and for your Highest Good – your heart is the centre of the Universe and contains all the answers to everything. It is connected to Infinite Wisdom. When you align with your heart and your Higher Power, not only will you receive what you asked for; you will also receive so much more – untold good with blessings and extras. The Universe is infinitely giving, loving and creative.

You are the receiver. When you realize that the power and resources of the Universe are limitless, and that there is an infinite well of abundance, you will feel naturally more relaxed and open to receiving. Nobody loses when you receive. The Universe is abundant and there is always an infinite supply of creativity and resources. The Universe can magic things out of thin air that previously weren't even in existence. There is enough for everyone, and more – the supply is endless. The Universe's well of creativity is constantly regenerating, renewing, recycling and re-forming. It is made of pure, Prima raw Materia Energy and is infinitely creating and expanding throughout eternity.

There aren't even any limits to what the Universe can create – and it loves to create! The Universe loves to expand itself, explore and fulfil itself though the manifestation and fulfilment of your wishes and

Paradise Is a State of Mind

desires. It planted them in your heart in the first place; because the Universe wishes to expand itself via creating new things, people, places and experiences. The joy of the Universe is creation, fulfilment and expansion. Because the Universe is Love, it requires a partner to do this with – this partner is you.

The Universe can and does create from thin air anything you want, even things you think can't be possible or even exist – it is nothing to the Universe. The Universe does not care. It draws upon your imagination and materializes things that weren't even previously in existence, so do not be afraid to ask for *anything* you want! There are no limits.

Know that the Universe is infinitely loving and creative, it loves you and you are one with it, and it is unlimited! The more you receive, the more you can give to everybody else. The more you receive, the more you have to give. A full cup overflows and gives to others. The more you receive and the happier you are, the more positive vibrations you put out into the world and uplift everyone around you! Claim your good now, knowing that the more good you receive, the more the entire world also receives!

A lot of people feel they have to give in order to balance out the receiving side of the equation. This is a myth! The Universe already takes care of the giving side of the equation. The Universe will use you as a Divine conduit to bless others. It is important that you just take care of the receiving – **your** receiving – first. When you allow and open up your own receiving channels, you naturally become a conduit for the divine and loving energy of the Universe, which will naturally inspire you to give and help others at points where it is best – in accordance with the Universe's Divine Plan! The Universe knows exactly how everything fits together in Creation, and knows exactly how to express itself through giving and receiving between people perfectly. When you leave the how of the giving equation up to the Universe, the outcome is always optimal and for the Highest Good of all! So connect to the powerful, loving Life Source Energy, experience and allow yourself to feel the joy of receiving and allow your own good to overflow and overfill your life first!! Give to others if it genuinely does already feel good, and know that the Universe is ultimately the best, highest, most generous and most loving decision-maker for distributing your gifts back!

Paradise Is a State of Mind

~•RECEIVING AFFIRMATIONS•~

- I radiate love and positivity, and pure, powerful good energy!

- I receive nothing but positive, pure, loving, rich abundant energy.

- I am a powerful, irresistible magnet for all good!

- I am a powerful magnet for luck, love, good fortune and outrageous blessings!

- I am a magnet for love, respect, adoration and admiration.

- I am a magnet for love, respect and appreciation.

- I am a magnet for untold wealth, success and abundance!

- I am a magnet for endless wealth, joy and prosperity.

- I am a magnet for endless wealth and Paradise.

-THE GIVER-

- I am a magnet for endless bliss and Paradise.

- I am a powerful magnet for the very best in life.

- I am a magnet for endless happiness and abundance.

- I am a magnet for endless joy and fulfilment.

- My love and joy are overflowing. My wealth and good are overflowing.

- The love in my heart overflows and expands and radiates out through the world. I receive immeasurable, boundless love and Paradise in return.

- I am a magnet for love and romance.

- I am a magnet for loving, fulfilling, exciting happy relationships.

- I am a magnet for loving, mutually fulfilling, flowing blissful relationships.

- I am a magnet for love, friendships, positivity and laughter!

Paradise Is a State of Mind

- I am a magnet for the very best friends. My life is so fun!

- I am a magnet for fun and love!

- I am a magnet for amazing times! My life is made up of the most exciting, fun, eventful, blissful happy positive experiences!

- My life is pure Paradise. I am always in the Present moment. My life is one fulfilling, love-filled paradisiacal moment after another.

- I am blessed with loving, fulfilling relationships.

- I have the very best people in my life.

- I am a lucky powerful magnet for the very best people, places, circumstances and events always.

- I receive never-ending, exquisite, radiant perfect health and bliss.

- I love and am proud of my gorgeous, glowing, exuberant radiant health!

- Love and joy fill my entire body.

-THE GIVER-

- My body is made of love, light and the highest positive vibrations! My body is filled with transcendent light and radiates positive, love-filled energy.

- I am proud of my perfect and gorgeous health.

- I love and approve of my body.

- I love and approve of myself! I am my own ideal.

- I am so grateful for the gift of my perfect body and my amazing heart, mind and soul!

- There is no-one like me. I am full of love and appreciation for myself.

- I am always receiving endless self-confidence, power, and fulfilment with myself from the Universe!

- The Universe gives me deep appreciation and adoration for my*self*, the most extravagant, rich, abundant gorgeous blessings and an entire life rich and saturated with love wherever I go.

- Life blesses me for all of eternity. The blessings and good are endless.

Paradise Is a State of Mind

- Life adores me. I am so lovingly taken care of!

- I am constantly showered with the most beautiful, breathtaking, awe-inspiring gorgeous blessings from the Universe! Life is vast, supernatural and limitless and it *loves* me.

- I am the happy and willing receiver of the generous, lavish abundance the Universe has for me.

- I am a joyful and ever-grateful recipient of the Universe's astonishing love and boundless blessings for me.

- Life loves me so much. The love and blessings are overwhelming.

- I am moved to tears by the Universe's generosity and goodness. The Universe is infinitely loving and jaw-droppingly abundant, and I am the centre of its affections.

- I am amazed with awe and wonder at the miraculous blessings, gifts and good the Universe showers down on me.

-THE GIVER-

- My receiving is unlimited! I am the unlimited receiver of an unbelievably kind, loving, generous, infinite, abundant Universe.

- There is only good in my life. My life is Paradise; never-ending Heaven on Earth.

- I am deeply grateful for all I receive.

- My life is awe-inspiring, serendipitous, magical, breathtaking and wondrous.

- My life is miraculous, never-ending bliss and Flow.

- I am cocooned in the loving, blissful radiant Energy of Life.

- I am swept off my feet daily with the most over-the-top miracles and sweet, happy surprises.

- It is incredible how much the Universe loves me.

- Everything positive, loving and good falls upon me.

- I am a magnet for only the very best life has to offer!

- I love and trust Life! I am open to the mystery, wonders, blessings and adventures of the Universe.

Paradise Is a State of Mind

- Countless ecstatic surprises and limitless joy lie before me.

- I am a radiant, powerful irresistible magnet for lucky events, people, places and circumstances!

- I am always in the perfect place in the divine right time.

- Amazing opportunities come my way daily.

- Things always work out for me in the most magical, impressive, beautiful unpredictable ways.

- Everything falls into place perfectly and in accordance with the divine right plan.

- The most loving, exciting, positive, helpful, inspiring, fun soul people fill my life!

- I am always receiving more good than I ever imagined or thought possible!

- The Universe brings me everything I desire and so much more!

- I am eternally, ever-grateful to Life! I am filled with love, gratitude, joy and Oneness. I radiate joy,

-THE GIVER-

gratitude, love and Oneness out to the Universe and I receive only love, gratitude, joy and Oneness back.

- My live is a living Paradise, a living Heaven on Earth.

- I am in a joyful, loving, blissful relationship with Life! I am the Source of Love and Paradise. Paradise is within me. Paradise is all around me. I *am* Paradise. I receive never-ending Paradise and Good.

Paradise Is a State of Mind

3.

-ABUNDANCE IS THE LOVE OF THE UNIVERSE-

Money is a form of the Universe's love for you, but money is not even real! It is intangible forms of Energy that we attempted to make appear real by creating coins, banknotes, gold, online banking, etc. Nevertheless, the Universe loves using these manmade channels to bless us with money! Money comes *through* people, but it is actually always coming *from* the Universe. The money comes from the Universe, which inspires people to give you money for whatever reason. This is also true in cases where people do not appear to be directly involved! For example, if you find money in the street 'randomly', know that it came from the Universe.

The Universe loves abundance, riches and money! The Universe loves luxury, wealth, beauty, comfort, freedom and harmony! Even if you did not specifically ask for money to the Universe, if you connected to the high-vibrational energy of Oneness with the Universe,

- ABUNDANCE IS THE LOVE OF THE UNIVERSE-

gratitude and Love, it is 99% probability that you will find yourself being surprised with unexpected financial blessings and success! This is because the energy of Love loves money; it is very fun for the Universe to play with and expand itself through money! Money is a form of the Universe's love for you. Material abundance, fulfilment and luck follow Positivity.

The Universe also multiplies itself – i.e. Love – through money. When you are vibrating at a very high frequency, Love moves through you, and as Love multiplies itself out in the world and between people, money also blesses others and uplifts the world! Money can always be used for Good. With money, we can buy organic, clean and healthy foods, contribute to the causes we love (e.g. veganism) via purchases, donate generously to the causes we support, connect with and share experiences with friends, bless and treat others to food, drinks or small gifts, bless others with larger gifts, and pay more for things that people have spent a lot of heart and effort into creating, compensating them more for their services! It is *highly* spiritual and abundant to have money!

All the Love and Good in the Universe wants you to have money! You are a beloved child of the Universe and Life *wants* you to be safe, relaxed, and deeply appreciating and delighting in the very best it has to offer!! Life has given you the key to receiving its

Paradise Is a State of Mind

unlimited abundance – your own power of choice of focus of energy frequency you choose to tune in to! It really is that simple. In the past, you may have blocked yourself off from abundance by buying into negative thoughts, but now you have every power of choice and focus in the Universe to tune in to and create a new, different, far better, more harmonious and exciting positive reality!! You can be as abundant, rich and wealthy as you choose – and free! Freedom, joy and prosperity accompany the Love energy of the Universe. Riches and lavish abundance are part of the frequency and energy of Love, and so they are found coexisting and intertwining with Love and joy. Your soul family – friends, colleagues, lovers, family and people you will meet wherever you go – are reflections of the vibrations of Love and Abundance. The Universe is only Love and Good, and so as you tune into the frequency of joyful Abundance, you will attract and connect with people who are on the exact same wavelength as you; who reflect and manifest the vibration of your heart and your loving, joyful connection with Abundant Source! If you are worried about leaving anyone behind as you increase your relationship to Flow and Abundance, let that go. When you increase your own happiness and abundance, your soul friends, lovers, family, etc. will also amplify their abundance and prosperity connection and grow along with you! Your soul family will also be loving and open and receptive to the Abundance and Good of the Universe. You will not

- ABUNDANCE IS THE LOVE OF THE UNIVERSE-

even have to say one word. The Universe brings you to the perfect people who match your loving Abundance vibration and who mirror your love with Source.

You do not need to know how your abundance is coming! All you need to do is have an idea of what you want, know that the Universe will bring it to you and feel grateful to the Universe that it is already manifesting!! You do not need to know how – it will happen for you in the most surprising, delightful ways – way better than you even imagined!! The Universe knows much better than you the infinite ways to bring you your desires and what will fulfil you and make you happy. It loves you, wants to surprise you and to sweep you off your feet! Inspired actions will come, but they will be fun, easy and joyful and you probably will not even realize you were taking inspired action most of the time until you look back!! This is what makes the process so fun and exciting. There really is no point even trying to work out how it will happen either, because 99.9% of the time, even if you think you know how something will happen, the Universe will circumvent your expectations and it will come in a way you never foresaw anyway – so trust that the Universe is working happily and tirelessly behind the scenes to bring you back your perfect match! This is the Universe's stage to show off. The Universe is the ultimate creator and performer, and every performer loves to exceed their own expectations and impress

Paradise Is a State of Mind

and wow their audience!

I think the reason why we can never really predict the way our dreams will realize is because the Universe loves creativity, originality and spontaneity. If we knew how everything would happen it would be boring!! Boring for us and for the Universe. **Let life surprise you! The very best things in life happen unexpectedly.**

- ABUNDANCE IS THE LOVE OF THE UNIVERSE-

~.ABUNDANCE AFFIRMATIONS.~

- I love money! I am an open channel for receiving money.

- I love receiving! The Universe pours money down on me. I gratefully and joyfully receive! I *deserve*.

- The Universe is abundant, infinite and loves to shower me with limitless good. The Universe loves to surprise me/make me happy/spoil me.

- The Universe uses money to demonstrate its love for me. Money *is* love from the Universe.

- My bank accounts are full and overflow with riches!

- The Universe has *so* much money. Whatever I take; whether multi-millions or billions, it is nothing to the Universe.

Paradise Is a State of Mind

- The Universe uses money lavishly and abundantly to demonstrate our connection. Money is love from the Universe.

- I always have so much money and abundance. I live in freedom, prosperity and joy.

- I enjoy having mountains and avalanches of abundance!

- My abundance is never-ending, ever-increasing, endless wealth and a permanence of overflow. I live in a limitless sea of joy, abundance and riches.

- I feel so lavish, rich and abundant! I love and adore money, and money loves me 10x more back. Life is so fun. I am always taken care of.

- More and more money is always coming into my life, and it is mine to keep. My prosperity is always increasing, my wealth is always building. I live in permanent prosperity, wealth, luxury and abundance.

- I live in permanent happiness, peace, security, luxury and bliss. Money is always there for me, and

- ABUNDANCE IS THE LOVE OF THE UNIVERSE-

me and my loved ones are always safe and taken care of. Money, i.e. the Universe, loves me and protects me. I am grateful to money and the Universe for its constant presence in my life.

- I spend lavishly and luxuriously, and I always receive 5-10x more income than my expenditure circulating out! I am always in Receiving mode. The Universe really loves me and I radiate happiness, abundance, luxury, bliss, fulfilment and peace. I live in a blissful cocoon of Radiance, Joy and Love.

- Money is always coming into my life casually and faithfully on a weekly, monthly, yearly basis, always in impressive, generous and extravagant amounts! My income is amazing and I receive money all the time from unexpected, surprising and happy sources.

- I love my wealth and abundance! It's so fun and hot to be abundant and successful. I radiate success, fun, money, abundance and fulfilment. I get paid handsomely – an absolute *fortune* – to do what I love; what sets my soul on fire – and am *exceptional* at it!!

Paradise Is a State of Mind

- Paradise is abundance; bliss; Extra. The Universe always gives me *more*. Paradise is fulfilment.

- Paradise is abundance, Extra, *more*. Paradise is fulfilment with extras and additional blessings I'd never even thought of or asked for. The Universe is always giving *more*. The Universe expands by me receiving.

- God is the Giver of all things and I am the receiver. The Giver expands by the giving and the more I receive, the more the Universe expands and rejoices. The joy of the Universe is expansion, creation and fulfilment.

- The more I allow myself to receive, the more the Universe gets to fulfil itself, grow and expand. When I receive more, the Universe rejoices for it expands into new desires and creations. It is an endless cycle of giving, creation, expansion and fulfilment.

- I am so safe in the universe. I am loved eternally by All of Creation.

- The universe is made of Love and abundance. Love and joy are intertwined through all the atoms of the

- ABUNDANCE IS THE LOVE OF THE UNIVERSE-

universe, and I am surrounded by it. The universe vibrates with joy, love and harmony. Peace and bliss surround me. I am loved and supported wherever I go.

- Life is generous, abundant, loving and full of joy. There is nothing but peace and bliss in the universe.

- I am surrounded at all times by loving, harmonious soul people. My soul people (friends, family, lover(s)), are loving, fun, abundant, rich, high-vibrational and heart-based! My soul people understand me and are like-minded. We vibrate on the same wavelength. My soul people also vibrate at the level of Love and Good. My own love and positive connection with Abundant Source is mirrored back to me.

- Abundance and Love follow me wherever I go and permeate my very being and existence. I am Love, Joy, Abundance and Harmony. We are one.

- I am meant to have it *all*. I am wildly, *wildly* wealthy, abundant, rich, prosperous and successful. I have extravagant wealth, abundance, luxury, fun, beauty

Paradise Is a State of Mind

and happiness. I live a rich, love-filled and fulfilling life! I have the very best that Life has to offer. I deserve and accept.

- I am very thankful to The Universe. I have abundance, prosperity and harmony.

- I live in peace and bliss with who I want to be with, where I want, doing what I want. My days are filled with endless bliss and Paradise.

- I am at home and perfectly comfortable – familiar – with vast sums of money, billions. I am a billionaire. Abundance is my destiny.

- I do so much good with my money. I am a shining Light in the world.

- I am a positive Influence and a transmitter of high vibrations and Radiant Light. I uplift everyone I meet.

- Wealth, money and abundance are good. The Universe is Good. There is nothing but Love and Light.

- There is always more Good. Source is limitless, never-ending and never runs out. Paradise is

- ABUNDANCE IS THE LOVE OF THE UNIVERSE-

limitless. There is always more and more Paradise and exciting new experiences ahead.

4.

-THE STAR OF THE SHOW-

Whatever you choose as your career and success in life is what you create.

Whether you choose good or bad for yourself, the Universe will unconditionally support you in whatever you do. If you focus on believing and thinking you are no good, unsuccessful, not supported, overworked and undercompensated, etc., then this is exactly what you'll create!! The Universe loves you enough to take you at your word and follow your command. It is really us that have the power to create our own circumstances – including our own successes and financial realities!!

It is very fun and empowering to realize your success is in your own hands! Whatever you choose, you create. Your Power is in your tongue!! The words you speak will create your experiences. When you honestly believe and choose the frequency that you are loved, valued and adored at work, that you have your best work soul family who adore you, and that work is a joy and full of love – then this is what you'll create!! If you

-THE STAR OF THE SHOW-

choose to believe that you are highly sought-after wherever you go, always employed by the best in your industry, and that you always get the top jobs and have multiple offers at a time... then guess what!? When you choose to believe that work is play, that you are always deeply fulfilled at work, and that you get to express your unique talents and gifts at every job/booking/client, then this is exactly what will materialize. The Universe doesn't judge whatever you choose as 'good' or 'bad' – it just lovingly supports what you put out. There really is nothing limiting our own successes apart from ourselves.

It might be hard to believe at first, because for so long it can seem as if there really was something doing 'it' to us. For example, in society there is an idea that we are 'job-seekers', rather than the higher-vibrational truth that we are *magnetic* to jobs, and that any job would be just as lucky to have us, as we would be to have it! Another false paradigm in society is that it is normal to work hard and toil for minimum wage at a job we hate. These are all just illusions arising from the world of scarcity and low vibrations!! They are falsehoods created at the level of *Maya* (the Sanskrit word for illusion) and separation. In the reality of Truth, Love and Power, which you can access through the key of your own higher vibrations, everything flows *for* you and in Divine harmony! As you enter the reality of Love and Oneness, everything and everyone is only here to

Paradise Is a State of Mind

help you. People love you, respect you, and see your unique work's value! Everybody benefits from being together. The Universe brings together the perfect people at the perfect time and in the perfect way, who all benefit from being with each other. There is only Divine harmony, Flow and success. You really do live in the Paradise of your own creation.

In the book *Transcending the Levels of Consciousness* by David R. Hawkins, Hawkins presents his 'Scale of Consciousness'; a tool that measures the vibrational Power of emotions from lowest to highest! The scale ranges all the way from 0 to 1000, with 0 representing the lowest state of consciousness (death), and 1000 representing the highest (enlightenment). The lowest vibrational states up from death include shame (20), apathy (50) and fear (100). Love (500), Joy (540) and Peace (600) are amongst the highest vibrational states of consciousness. The lower states of consciousness have weak vibrational Power, and an individual in these states creates reality paradigms of survival, struggle and 'getting by.' In such states, the energetic field of a person transmitting these vibrations is contracted, weak and ineffectual. Any influence these states do produce on the world are very minimal, and weakly negative. The lower states are associated with selfishness and victimhood. However, the further we move up the scale, towards the levels of Love and above, the more gravitas and vibrational Power our positive states yield. Towards the levels of Love, Joy and Enlightenment, our energy fields expand massively, and the influence we have on the world is profound, tremendous and reaches the entire planet. The higher states of consciousness are selfless, and empowered. The more Powerful we become, the more we uplift everyone around us and create reality paradigms of Flow and Transcendence.

At the Love level, when you are feeling happy, fulfilled, and confident in yourself and the unique value of what you have to offer, everyone else is also uplifted, and benefits from your personal success as a Whole! The energy of Love is so inclusive and harmonizing; that anything created at this level – including your own unique fulfilment, personal success and happiness – is magic for the Highest Good of all! Your success somehow magically benefits everybody else's. In the Business of Divine Love, there is only mutual harmony, cooperation and mutual success for *all*.

You can choose *exactly* what you want, knowing that in doing so you are contributing towards creating a living Paradise on Earth for the entire planet! You are free to create absolute freedom living where you want to live, with whom you want to be with, doing what deeply fulfils you on every level. Your reality really is just what you make it! Think thoughts of love, success, joy, passion, excitement, abundance, fulfilment, freedom,

Paradise Is a State of Mind

never-ending safety, security and bliss, and this is what your world becomes! A great affirmation is: Every day at work is fun, joy and bliss! You want to feel loved, joyful and fulfilled at work; having fun and feeling the love of the Universe through your work and through the people you work with! Prosperity goes hand-in-hand with the love of the Universe; therefore the happier and more fulfilled you are at work, the more the Abundance (i.e. the love of the Universe) naturally follows!!

The Universe will lovingly, passionately create a happy, joyous and fulfilling work-life for you, just as easily as it may've created any unsatisfactory or unhappy experiences before! It really is impartial – and so when you choose happiness, fulfilment and abundance at work, the Universe will just as easily and happily create that for you, with as much passion and zeal as it ever created anything before!! The Universe is very loving and fervent in its creations, and so it will be very creative and attentive to detail when shaping your beautiful new reality to match your new career/success vibrations!! As you affirm success, prosperity, joy, fun and bliss in your work life, you will be met with an endless stream of people, circumstances and events that support and perfectly reflect back to you your new success and abundance thinking!!

What you put out is what you will shape and create in

-THE STAR OF THE SHOW-

your world. The more love, passion, joy, success, self-belief and unique value you claim for yourself with your words, the more the Universe will lovingly create that and bring it back to you. Allow your own fulfilment now! Create your own incredible success, bliss, fun, joy and happiness at work internally with your affirmations – and watch with astonishment and joy as Life lovingly brings it back to you! The happier, more successful and more fulfilled you feel on the inside, and the more you feel Life lovingly supporting you in doing what you love, the more connected and open you will be to receiving the love, support and rewards of the Universe!

Paradise Is a State of Mind

~•SUCCESS AFFIRMATIONS•~

- I live the life of my dreams.

- I am extremely happy and successful!

- I thrive and succeed at everything I do.

- I am out outrageously successful!

- I have the magic touch.

- I am Love and Positivity.

- I leave magic wherever I go!

- Everybody loves to be around me.

- I am highly sought-after, cherished and valued in my industry.

- I am recognized as a treasure and a unique, diamond prize in my industry.

- I am the very best in my industry!

-THE STAR OF THE SHOW-

- My natural talents pour forth.

- I love what I do, and am extremely talented and creative at it!

- I do what I love, what sets my soul on fire, and I am extremely recognized, rewarded and supported along my path.

- Everyone sees me as the must-have in my industry. I am highly valued and respected.

- I work with the very best people in my industry, who value and cherish my unique talents, and nurture and develop my potential. My potential explodes tenfold.

- I am always improving. I am always reaching new heights.

- I always only ever move up and up, and become better and better!

- I love myself and my unique creative talents, skills and gifts. I am utterly unique and worthy.

- Anybody is just as lucky to have me/work with me, as I them!

Paradise Is a State of Mind

- I am a leader in my industry. I have an unrivalled depth of wisdom, knowledge, skills and potential/innate talent.

- Everybody appreciates my value. I love what I do and am **great** at it.

- I am outlandishly successful!! I am extraordinary, a top 5%er and an outlier.

- I live at the extraordinary, peak level of existence.

- I have a unique, starry destiny!

- The Universe loves me and supports me in everything I do.

- I am endlessly guided by the loving Universe throughout eternity.

- I trust the Universe. I am constantly led somewhere very special.

- There is a unique, grand, starry, Higher Plan for me.

- I love and trust myself. I follow my own intuition.

- I earn a fortune doing what I absolutely love!

-THE STAR OF THE SHOW–

- I earn a fortune doing what sets my soul on fire.

- I am so happy. I am in a cocoon of Love and Bliss. The Universe deeply fulfils me and supports me as I do what I love.

- I am deeply, *deeply* fulfilled by my work. I create the most unique, invaluable, breathtaking bodies of work/works of art/creations!

- I feel deeply fulfilled in the universe. I feel one with Life.

- Life always gets better and better for me. I move into my Greater Good always.

- Everything is wonderful. I live in the Paradise of my own creation.

- All of the Love of the Universe supports me. I am endlessly being guided to where I need to be.

- Life loves me, and supports everything I do. My creations are lovingly, effortlessly supported and guided.

Paradise Is a State of Mind

- My success is ever-increasing, ever-expanding and always reaching new heights. My income from doing what I love constantly increases.

- I earn more and more money from doing what I love, and more and more appreciation and respect. I am deeply fulfilled, and confident.

- I love being me and what I create. I have a unique value and many things to bring to this world.

- I am outrageously abundant and financially successful! I live a life of utter freedom doing what I love, with the most loving, best people and in endless joy and prosperity. Life really is a Paradise of my own making.

- I see love everywhere. Paradise is all around me, moving through me and radiating out from me! I live in never-ending joy, bliss and fun!!

- Everything I experience raises my awareness to a new level, and evolves me as a person to the next, best version of my Self. I love, welcome and enjoy challenges, because I know they only ever make me more beautiful and Powerful.

-THE STAR OF THE SHOW-

- I have innate wisdom and offerings to leave behind in this world.

- Love follows me wherever I go, and permeates everything I do! I create a life filled with love, prosperity and joy. I create a Love-filled reality that vibrates with success, confidence, mutual benefit and harmony.

- I feel so good about myself! I love who I am and what I do! I am deeply supported by the loving, abundant Universe.

- Everything I do is supported tenfold by the Universe. The Universe is passionate to co-create with me.

- I love who I am and what I do, and I feel deeply at peace. I know that everything is always working out for the Highest Plan of all.

- The happier, more fulfilled and more confident I feel at work, the more everybody benefits!! My success is prosperous for the Highest Good of all.

- The happier, more successful and more confident I feel, the more money I make! The more I support

Paradise Is a State of Mind

and believe in myself, the more the Universe supports and believes in me. My own love and respect for myself comes back to me mirrored.

- Love follows my tongue! Whatever I speak is what I create. The energy of Love manifests the most loving circumstances, people, projects, places, products, services and events in complete harmony for the Highest Good of all.

- When I speak success from the energy of Love, I manifest success carrying the vibrations and energies of my own Love back to me.

- The more I believe in myself, my self-worth and unique gifts of what I have to offer, the more the reality of other people and the Universe mirror that back to me through people, places, circumstances and events.

- Everything is in Divine Order. Everything is always moving toward my Highest Good and greatest potential. I am always fulfilled, loving and loved.

- I enjoy everything Life has to offer me and every opportunity brought to me. I know that what I give out, I get back. I give back appreciation,

-THE STAR OF THE SHOW—

gratitude and joy in the moment and I manifest back happiness, creation and fulfilment in the moment.

- The more bliss, fun and success I give out, the more bliss, success and fun I create. Every positive energy I give out comes back to me mirrored. The Universe supports the vibration of the positive energies I give out a tenfold-hundredfold.

- The Universe supports every iota of positivity I give out hundredfold. What I give out positively is always coming back to me a hundred, thousand times over. I live in the Paradise of my own creation.

- The Universe lovingly supports every bit of positivity I put out tenfold-thousandfold, eternally. Every bit of my Highest Good and loving creation is supported and matched tenfold-thousandfold.

- Only love, success, deep, utter fulfilment and joy come to me!

5.

-WHEN IT IS ALL FINISHED, YOU WILL DISCOVER IT WAS NEVER RANDOM.-

There is an ancient Hindu & Buddhist concept called dharma, which is divine purpose, destiny and one's calling! Each one of us is here to fulfil our own unique purpose in our lifetime here on Earth, and our longings and callings for what we want to do come directly from our heart. Dharma comes from the all-knowing, all-powerful unique Truth of your heart! The heart has an intricate knowledge of what everyone and everything is here to do, and how it all links together for the highest interests of everyone. I believe there is a grand Divine Plan for our lives, and each one of us plays a specific and unique role in Creation – by following our honest callings and pursuing our dreams. When we are true to ourselves and follow our passions, we allow our dreams to unfold before us and all around us, and we fulfil our unique role in the grand Divine Plan. The Universe needs us to follow our hearts, our passions, unique creativity and

-WHEN IT IS ALL FINISHED, YOU WILL DISCOVER IT WAS NEVER RANDOM.-

gifts because when we do so we light up the fire of All of Creation! The heart lies at the very centre of the Universe. The heart is the highest embodiment of Love, Truth, joy, passion and pure positive Life Force – high-vibrational, positive, pure, loving Source Energy.

It is a spiritual and divine truth that you are here to follow your own unique dreams and individual longings. The Universe has instilled a unique desire in your heart that is specific to you, because only you can fulfil it. The Universe wants and needs you to play your part in the Divine matrix of Creation. By following your own passions and what lights you up, you are contributing to Divine harmony and the fulfilment and expansion of the Universe!! The Universe's desires and your own unique, individual dreams are one and the same. Every wish you have in your heart comes from your Higher Self, who connects to the Grand Plan and All of Creation. The Universe does not make mistakes. Every single person who has an interest and desire for something is meant to pursue that dream; because it is their divine assignment. The Love and Harmony of the Divine Plan wants you to follow your dreams.

As you pursue your dreams and allow Life to unfold your path before you, you light up everyone you come into contact with, everyone you work with and associate with and everyone around you! We are all

Paradise Is a State of Mind

here to mutually benefit each other in a symbiosis. The Universe is living, breathing, organic and everything has a symbiotic relationship with one another. In the matrix of Divine Love and Harmony, we are all coexisting in harmony and for the highest evolution of the Universe. Our individual expansions, desires and fulfilment are all unique parts of a Whole.

The Universe will figure out for you, as you pursue things that may've seemed impossible, a way through obstacles and doorways will appear where there were only walls. This is what is meant by the infamous Joseph Campbell quote: 'Follow your bliss, and the Universe will open doors for you where there were only walls.' There is truly no impossible. What is meant for you will always be for you, regardless of any seeming competition (i.e. an illusion), age barriers, race barriers, socio-economic barriers, etc. Whatever your perceived limitation, it is non-existent and merely an illusion to the Universe. Whatever has been divinely assigned to you is destined to be attained by and realized through you, so relax!

As you accept that the Universe does indeed support your dharma, you begin to see the supportation of your dreams and desires unfolding wherever you go. You experience a lucky and opportune series of events and experiences, which will all lead you to the right place at the right time! Sure, there may be some dead ends,

-WHEN IT IS ALL FINISHED, YOU WILL DISCOVER IT WAS NEVER RANDOM.-

detours and reversals along the way, but in the end you will always reach your destination right on time! Any mis-tours you do take along your journey add up and contribute to the richness and fullness of who you become, and the depth and colour of your story.

I believe there is a Divine Order to everybody's life. Our dreams and desires realize at the perfect times and in the perfect sequence, and usually we as humans don't know how to put them together. This is where the Divine Mind of the Universe will always come through. There is Divine Order in Higher Intelligence and the Universe knows how to put things together and interweave things seamlessly where we do not. There is a Divine Flow, Harmony and Order to life and when you relax and trust in a Higher Power and the innate goodness of Life, you allow yourself to access the harmony of this flow.

When it is time for a dream to come true, a continual stream of opportunities and doorways will open for you where indeed, it may have seemed as if there were only walls! Let it in! Life is waiting for us to say yes to opportunity, positivity and prosperity. It is all available to us; it's just that sometimes we block it with our own negative thoughts. Do not buy into any external limited myths such as 'you are too old for this, too young for that, too short, too stupid, too *whatever*' – they are all just illusions – all fear is! Only Love and

Paradise Is a State of Mind

Truth exist on the higher-vibrational planes, and have only Good for you. Believe in yourself 110%, 120%, and 1000%. In Source's eyes, you are perfect and more than worthy, good enough and even superfluously innately equipped for your dreams!

If you do need anything additional to reach your goals, for example the acquisition of a new skill, language, piece of equipment, technical qualification, etc., then the means and method of obtention will be provided to you easily and effortlessly. This is also fun, exciting and part of the adventure as you will be adding to your skill-set and growing as a person along the way.

As we believe in ourselves and that the Universe supports our deepest heart's desires, we experience a world where our own self-belief and belief in the Universe comes back to us mirrored! Life is patiently waiting for us to say yes to our dreams, and when we let them in with the positive words we speak and the vibrations we give out, the Good coming to us is unstoppable!

You have a divine, sublime, loving Higher Power who is capable of *anything* and whose primary mission and purpose in life is to fulfil you, guide you, support you and assist you! You are always divinely guided, protected and led on your path.

53

-WHEN IT IS ALL FINISHED, YOU WILL DISCOVER IT WAS NEVER RANDOM.-

Be fearless in the pursuit of what sets your soul on fire. Your heart and soul work in tandem with the Divine Higher Plan – listen to your heart and trust *yourself*. Your intuition is always guiding you to exactly where you need to be at the perfect right time.

Paradise Is a State of Mind

~•DESTINY AFFIRMATIONS•~

- I am always divinely led, called to, and guided to my desires.

- My path unfolds effortlessly before me. I am the loving co-creator of my dreams with a loving, all-knowing Higher Power.

- As I follow my dreams and desires, I contribute to the grand unfolding of the Divine Higher Plan.

- Life endlessly supports the fulfilment of my desires and dreams. A continual series of jaw-dropping, beautiful coincidences and unbelievable events opens up for before me. I am effortlessly carried with The Flow to the realization of my deepest dreams!

- All of my heart's desires and deepest dreams are divinely fulfilled! I relax as I realize I am in tandem

-WHEN IT IS ALL FINISHED, YOU WILL DISCOVER IT WAS NEVER RANDOM.-

with the most loving, powerful Creator who wants only good for me!

- My deepest fulfilment benefits the Universe and All of Creation. I do my part in fulfilling the Divine Plan.

- I pursue my passions and my unique dreams and goals! I am fearless in the pursuit of what sets my soul on fire.

- I love and honour myself and my Divine calling! I believe in myself. There is no-one like me who can fulfil my unique role in the Whole of Creation.

- I love and rejoice in my bespoke talents and gifts! There is no-one like me. Only I can fulfil the role God has perfectly planned for me. Life has a unique, special purpose for me.

- We are all coexisting in a loving, harmonious co-collaboration to expand Love and Harmony as a Whole. I love life, and I fulfil and express myself creatively; as I do so I give others permission to do the same!

Paradise Is a State of Mind

- My success and deep fulfilment following my dreams lights up the entire planet. The more love, joy and happiness I feel deep in my soul, the higher vibrations I put out into the planet!

- We are all working together for love, peace and joy. The more joy I feel and the more I creatively express myself at work, the more joy and light I vibrate out into the world!

- My success, joy and happiness doing what I love is everybody's win!

- The fulfilment of my deepest wishes and desires brings joy and lights up the planet.

- The deepest expressions of my heart and soul create beauty, transcendence and love wherever I go.

- The fulfilment of my art and creativity/gifts/talents creates a body of light!

-WHEN IT IS ALL FINISHED, YOU WILL DISCOVER IT WAS NEVER RANDOM.-

- My works of art/creations/gifts light up, heal and expand the planet!

- My work/art/creative expression is pure love, high vibrations, transcendence and positivity.

- I am deeply, immensely fulfilled by everything that I do! My love and joy light up the planet! I live in a cocoon of Love, bliss and Oneness.

- I live in the passion and joy of my own love and fulfilment! What I give out comes back to me tenfold. This only works with positivity. When I give out love, self-belief and joyful gratitude for my talents and gifts, I receive it back to me mirrored in abundance wherever I go! Love, passion and bliss follow me wherever I go.

- I am one with all of Life. All of my deepest dreams and heart's desires are always divinely fulfilled. I am one with the Universe.

6.

-A CAT THAT ALWAYS LANDS ON THEIR FEET-

The luckier you believe you are, the luckier the energy you put out into the cosmos and the luckier the energy that comes back to you!! When you start to believe and radiate how lucky you are, you project an energy signal out into the universe that radiates that you are a positive, lucky and blessed person, who receives everything you want, and that life goes your way – reality bends in your favour and you are divinely guided and led in everything you do! You give out the energy that you are favoured by life and that all the forces in the universe come together to conspire for your Highest Good! Life is friendly, optimistic, fun, always gives you the best, and you are lucky and positive. You expect the best, and you get it!!

Exuding the energy of luck will incredibly boost your confidence, as when you know Life loves you, it is only natural that you start to feel good about yourself! How can you feel down on yourself when you know Life loves you and goes your way!?! Feeling lucky empowers you. It gives you the confidence to go for your goals, set extraordinary ambitions and aim high, believe in yourself and persist in the face of any obstacles!! Challenges and setbacks may happen, but you will more easily bounce them off – luck makes you extremely *resilient.*

If you ever feel bad about yourself, or feel you are having a losing streak, it often feels like you are unlucky or cursed! This can often translate into a feeling of being uncared for or even scorned by Life – or at the very least feeling unimportant or forgotten about! This is so far from the Truth of You. If you are still reading this book, you are probably an optimistic person who sets high (and even extraordinary) goals for yourself! Lucky people shrug off adversity more easily. It still hurts, of course, but they shake it off, keep going and believe in themselves!! Lucky people are winners; confident in their chances despite any external odds and ultimately know that success is theirs!! Luck directly correlates to self-belief.

The luckier you *believe* you are, the luckier you become. What you believe about yourself is what you tend to get back! This was scientifically proven with psychological studies performed by Professor Richard Wiseman, author of *The Luck Factor.* Wiseman's research found that lucky people *expect* to be lucky, and

Paradise Is a State of Mind

that creates a positive self-reinforcing loop! Projecting the energy of luck and self-belief allows you to go for opportunities most people don't go for, persist in the face of obstacles, and even use and turn around these obstacles to your advantage!! Having the 'luck filter' also filters your mental perception; allowing you to see all the ways things are working out for you, all the good in your life and occurring for you daily... and all the ways Life conspires to fulfil your dreams and make you come out a winner!! Having these mental blinkers on keeps your perception focused on all your own good luck; keeping you resilient!

I believe good luck also works energetically. You project out an 'I am lucky' energy and this energy goes out and finds lucky people, circumstances, places and events to match itself and return to you in like form, thus proving your point!! The more luck you put out, the more you get back. It really is that simple – like all the other principles covered in this book. Money, success, love, confidence, beauty, harmony, etc. – it all comes back to you multiplied when you believe in it, affirm it is who you are and what you get, and radiate it out! Luck is no exception.

Luck truly is one of the best and most fun energies you can create for yourself! Not only will it increase your confidence and self-esteem (because going for your goals, believing in yourself and that things always work

out for you increases your own positive feelings you
have about yourself!); you will also sail more easily
through life's challenges and come out a winner – and
always better off than before!! Lucky people take
unexpected things that happen to them and turn them
around to their advantage! There is an ancient parable
about a Chinese farmer that demonstrates this
perfectly:

The farmer experiences several incidences, all varying
in degrees of misfortune and fortune, and is wise
enough to wait patiently before passing judgement on
anything seemingly negative as 'bad'. For example, one
night his prize horse runs away, and his neighbours
comment on how unlucky he is. However, the wise
farmer, knowing better, quietly comments 'maybe.'
The next night, his prize horse returns with seven more
wild horses! The farmer not only has his original horse
back; he now also has seven more horses than before,
and it never would have happened if it weren't for the
initial 'unfortunate' event! Later, the neighbours
comment again on the farmer's seemingly bad luck,
when one of the seven horses throws the farmer's son
off itself and breaks the boy's leg in the process! Again,
in response to his neighbours' commiseration, the
farmer simply replies 'maybe.' A few days later, when
the army comes to enlist all the local young men in
military service, the farmer's son cannot join due to his
broken leg. All the other villagers' sons get enlisted and

Paradise Is a State of Mind

die in the battle. The farmer's previous 'bad luck' spares him his beloved son.

Every seemingly negative thing that happens to a lucky person gets turned in their favour into a blessing in disguise! This is a winner's attitude and the best way to receive life! Work to see the Divine harmony and hidden benevolence in life's challenges, and you will soon form a very loving world around you, where everything works out spectacularly for you! I actually believe that things are already always working out for us whether we believe it or not, but because the strength of the flow of good is directly correlated to how much we're letting it in, when we *expect* good luck, our positive expectations amplify the flow! Our positive beliefs and expectations allow the good to pour and rush in, rather than drip through minimally. Open your floodgates to receive the immense rivers of love, joy, abundance, good and luck Life has for you! When you lift the clouds of disbelief and negative expectation, the sunshine of Life and Positivity begin to dominate your mind – allowing all the good to pour in.

One of the best books I have ever read on luck is by British hypnotherapist Paul McKenna: *The 3 Things That Will Change Your Destiny Today!* In this book, McKenna reinforces that luck is a state of mind – that believing you are luckier sends out a vibrational energy of luck, bringing more luck back to you!! He also gives a very effective and powerful NLP (neuro-linguistic programming) visualization exercise designed to increase your luck! You can actually feel the lucky vibrations as you practice it! I highly recommend this book if you want to practice the vibration of luck. Practising luck affirmations is also an excellent practical method to increase your luck! There are luck affirmations included at the end of this chapter.

In summary: the more you expect things to go your way, the more you feel that Life loves you, the more you see yourself as lucky, and the more you love life, the luckier you get! These energies all come together to create a beautiful Flow. It feels so good to ride the wave of Luck and Fortune in life! When you consistently radiate powerful, positive, joyful and expectant energy, you build an energetic ocean full of love, kindness, positivity, luck and fortune! This quantum energy is teeming with waves of luck, love, positivity, synchronicity, fortune, opportunities, chance meetings, Divine Timing and serendipity!! This ocean will carry you through the choppiest ups and downs of life; always ensuring you come out radiant on top, your good luck and fortune dazzlingly intact and stronger than ever!! Any choppy or tumultuous waters will only make you luckier and stronger in the end!! Rougher seas create the most skilled sailors. Whether the waves are up or down, you will always be a winner. Life is eternally on your side.

Paradise Is a State of Mind

You are deeply loved and infinitely supported by this incredible Universe. Life wants you to win and is always conspiring for your Higher Good. There is an undercurrent of benevolence to life. The more you see and record Life loving you and the way things always work out for you, the more luck you exude and attract back into your life!

~.Attitudes to Increase Your Luck.~

1. Daily gratitude practice

Practicing a mindset of gratitude is one of the quickest, most powerful, potent and positive ways to put luck energy out into the universe!! Why? Because when you practise noticing and taking strong count of your blessings, you send out an emotional signature into the universe that says, 'Good things are always happening for me!!' I have noticed in my own life that when I deliberately practise cultivating feelings of gratitude, my entire life does become luckier! I think it is because when you practice noticing your blessings and all the daily good that Life brings, you can't help but soon feel luckier as you realize, 'Life really is on my side!'

Regularly observing how fortunate you are and celebrating your blessings with gratitude is a sure-fire, guaranteed fast-track to luck! I actually find the daily journal of recording your blessings that happened during that day to be the most effective way of increasing your luck – as you take note of all the good things that happen throughout the day, your brain is subconsciously recording all the ways Life comes up with *new* good for you every day to make you smile, improve your mood, boost your happiness and just brighten your day!! Gratitude enables us to see the miracles that surround us daily. It is an ongoing, magical energy. Life is there for you every day, bringing you new surprises – big and small – all the time! This is why I think it is important to keep a regular gratitude diary, so you record all the frequent luck that Life sends your way! And of course, the more you practise gratitude for your daily miracles, the more your energetic gratitude signature builds up and your luck gets stronger and stronger... bringing back even more to feel grateful and lucky about!!

2. Don't take anything personally

One of the most interesting things I have ever read is that optimists blame other people when things go wrong, rather than themselves!! On the other hand,

Paradise Is a State of Mind

when things go well, optimists attribute it to their own success rather than others' involvement!! Isn't that interesting!?! Meanwhile, pessimists do the exact opposite!! A pessimist blames themselves when things go wrong, and when things go right, they give others the credit! Luck and optimism go hand-in-hand. If you want to increase the amount of luck you experience, you must start thinking and acting like an optimist!! When things go wrong, especially in personal relationships, assume the fault lies with the other person and not you. Is this dangerous? Not really. Most people have the common sense to be reasonable and realistic about the part they have played in a given situation. But pessimistic or unlucky people tend to take it too far, and take *over*-responsibility. If you look back on examples in your own life, you will probably see that most of your emotional distress in personal relationships came from accepting far more responsibility than was rightfully yours – letting other people slide with treating you with less than you deserve because you somehow thought that it was your fault! Nothing could be further from the truth!! Most spiritual people really are too nice sometimes, and especially in romantic relationships, they do not accept the credit they deserve! So, the next time something does goes wrong, do be sensible and realistically look at your responsibility in the situation. However, if you are completely honest, doesn't it always seem that maybe you just got involved with someone who didn't quite deserve you or wasn't good enough for you in the first place!?! Being truthful with yourself about that, owning it and realizing you deserve so much better, allows you to free yourself to move on to new, better people who will treat you as good as you deserve!!

This is also true in friendships! A lot of the time, people outgrow each other! This is no great failure at all. Not every friendship or relationship is supposed to last. Of course there are heart bonds, soul friends and soulmates; these tend to be permanent lasting bonds that are very durable and forgiving. Aside from soulmates and soul friends though, most friendships and connections are designed to expire because of the transitory nature of life; life is always evolving and growing! With each new stage of life comes new people, new faces, new places, new growth, etc. It would be boring if it was always the same! So if people do leave your life, especially during a challenging period, know these weren't your people long-term, and new and even better people are coming in for you, that are more of a match to where you're going!! Remember, life is always getting better and better and moving towards your Highest Good and evolution. Do not

Paradise Is a State of Mind

hang onto people who were a match to a lower-vibrational version of you. Whoever is meant to be in your life will stay in your life – or, if they do leave, they will end up coming back without you forcing it! You will never need to fight or cling onto what or who is meant for you. Let fate play its hand. You are far too good to hang on to anybody, plus, the higher-vibrational version of you will be powerfully magnetic to new and better places, people, faces, situations and circumstances! Trust Life to always bring you to your Higher Good. If you look back on all the times you went through this before, you'll see all the times it worked out magically, serendipitously and beautifully for you in the end!! You always get to where you need to go, and life is always moving up towards new and better things. Be ridiculously optimistic.

3. <u>Eyes on the prize</u>

When you are going for a goal, whether it be a new job, career, place to live, a big move, a soulmate, etc. it is important to keep your eyes on the prize! Meaning, you have a goal and nothing and no-one on this Earth is getting in your way! That thing is yours, it has been divinely promised to you, and you're not stopping until you get it! Do not be deterred by any 'mirages' that don't work out. It is a bit like this... imagine you are crossing a desert. How slow or fast you cross that desert to get to your oasis is up to you! If you allow yourself to be distracted or hung up by anything that doesn't work out, it slows you down. On the other hand, if you keep your eyes on the prize – your goal and where you're going, no mirage can be fool enough to dissuade you! Your eyes are on the prize and it will work out for you. You will get what you want. When you keep your focus unwavering and fixed in this way, you will speed through the desert, reach your oasis quicker with less hitches, and anything unsatisfactory or untoward that comes towards you along the way will just bounce right off you!! Eyes on the prize and keep moving! Nothing stops you until you get what you want.

Paradise Is a State of Mind

~•LUCK AFFIRMATIONS•~

- I am outrageously lucky.

- I am outlandishly lucky.

- I am lavishly, ridiculously lucky.

- I have incredible good fortune.

- My luck is incredible.

- I am the luckiest person I know!

- My luck is outstanding!

- I am outlier lucky.

- My good luck is extraordinary!

- My good luck is astonishing.

- I always land on my feet!

-A CAT THAT ALWAYS LANDS ON THEIR FEET-

- I am jaw-droppingly lucky.

- My luck is admirable.

- I have unbelievable luck.

- Things always work out for me.

- I am bold and fearless.

- I am brave and intrepid.

- I always go for what I want.

- I am courageous and a risk-taker.

- I love and enjoy challenges! They make me stronger and always result in a doubling or tripling of my good luck!!

- I know that things always work out for me. There is benevolence in every challenge.

- I turn every experience into an opportunity to grow! I am always blessed by challenges.

- Life is on my side.

- Everything happens for my Highest Good.

Paradise Is a State of Mind

- The Universe is on my side.

- I am resilient and fearless.

- I am daring and intrepid.

- I aim extraordinarily high and I achieve extreme, extraordinary things! I love and am proud of myself.

- I am extremely successful, a risk-taker and an outlier.

- I am very resilient and persevere in the face of obstacles!

- Fortune favours the brave! The winds of fortune are always turning in my favour.

- I set sail on the seas of endless good luck and fortune!

- I am always riding on the wings of Fortune.

- I am blessed by the gods.

- I believe in myself, and Life believes in me.

-A CAT THAT ALWAYS LANDS ON THEIR FEET-

- My good luck comes from my self-belief and my belief in the goodness of Life. I trust Life to always give me what I want.

- I love myself and I deserve the very best in life.

- Life is always working in my favour. I am a beloved child of the Universe, and Life loves me very much.

- Everything happens for my Higher Good.

- Life is always moving towards my greatest growth and highest potential. I am always being fast-tracked to my Highest Good.

- Life is benevolent, generous, abundant and loving.

- Everything happens **for** me.

- My life overflows with incredible, seamless good luck and fortune, astonishing synchronicity and the most fortuitous circumstances and events.

- My entire life flows together seamlessly, magically and harmoniously.

- I am deeply, unfathomably loved by this infinite Universe.

Paradise Is a State of Mind

- Everything always works out for me and in my favour.

- Life loves me deeply. I am so loved and cared for by Life!

- Life always conspires for me to reach my deepest, truest and most extraordinary dreams.

- I always achieve my wildest dreams and most extraordinary goals.

- Life is on my side always.

- I am an outlier and extraordinary. I believe in myself.

- I always win in life. I always reach my goals and highest potential. I am always learning and growing.

- My life is always moving into greater and greater levels of Good.

- Life is always getting better and better for me. There is no end to the good I can create!

-A CAT THAT ALWAYS LANDS ON THEIR FEET-

- I believe in myself and achieve extraordinary things.

- Every experience I have benefits me. I am always using my experiences for growth, and I always come out the other side 3-5x stronger and better off than before!!

- Every failure is a stepping stone to where I'm meant to be.

- Life always ends up magically and beautifully working out in my best interests and in my favour!

- I have the magic touch. I radiate lucky energy.

- I have the golden touch. I emblazon magic, lucky gorgeous energy wherever I go!

- Everything works out for me exceptionally.

- I am fantastically lucky.

- I radiate magic, luck and success! I turn every experience into a hidden blessing.

- I am my own best friend. I love myself.

- I am remarkably lucky, patient and perseverant.

Paradise Is a State of Mind

- I believe in myself and admire myself. I am resilient and optimistic.

- I keep my eyes on the prize and where I'm going. I don't stop until I get what I want.

- I am grateful for every experience in life.

- I look for the good in any situation. There is always something to be thankful for.

- There is a silver lining to every cloud!

- I am otherworldly lucky. My luck is supernatural.

- I create my own luck and magic.

- I radiate dazzling, gorgeous, glowing magnetic luck!

- I always win at life and I love myself!

- I am incredibly talented, brave, resourceful, resilient and gifted in my attitude. I don't give up.

- I am an irresistible magnet for golden opportunities!!

-A CAT THAT ALWAYS LANDS ON THEIR FEET-

- I am magnetic to the *best*, most outlandish opportunities.

- I am a magnet for the most incredible, luckiest people, places, circumstances and events!

- Only the best comes my way! Everything good comes to me.

- Everything always works out to my advantage.

- I am destined for greatness.

- I am always receiving the very best life has to offer me! Everything happens *for* me.

- I see the good in everything that happens to me! I feel so safe in life.

- I am endlessly supported by the loving Universe.

- Challenges are only here to strengthen me, help me and prosper me further.

- Life loves me infinitely. Everything only ever happens *for* me and to fast-track me to more blessings, my higher growth and even greater Good.

Paradise Is a State of Mind

- There is only good in the Universe.

- On the other side of fear, lies challenge, growth and excitement.

- I am always safe in the flow of life. I let the flow carry me where I'm meant to go, knowing there is a Divine rhythm and Higher harmony to life.

- Everywhere I go, good luck is waiting for me around every corner!

- I sail on the seas of life with winds of outrageous prosperity and good fortune! Waves of opportunity are abundant.

- I am divinely blessed and protected wherever I go.

- I am on a hero's journey. I love and believe in myself!!

- My belief in myself and in Life is unwavering! I am strong and determined.

- I conquer everything that comes my way and always come out stronger and richer. Everything always happens *for* me.

-A CAT THAT ALWAYS LANDS ON THEIR FEET-

- My life goes from strength to strength, win to win and blessing to further blessing always!

- Life is a series of serendipitous, gorgeous accidents, delightful eventful coincidences, abundantly, gorgeously-blessed events and fortunate incidents one after another!! My life is a Flow of luck and delight.

- I float on a sea of serendipitous good luck and fortune.

- I am divinely lucky and blessed.

- I am always receiving everything I ask for and so much more. I receive the very best life has to offer always. I attain every goal, every desire and wish for myself and Life loves and supports me.

- I endlessly float on a sea of good fortune, beautiful blessings and auspicious prosperity! Life loves me.

7.

-IF YOU BELIEVE IN YOURSELF, ANYTHING IS POSSIBLE-

This chapter is about challenges, a positive attitude, resilience and self-belief! Lucky and successful people have a way of handling challenges that is different from the norm. For a lucky or optimistic person a challenge is an opportunity and handled with a very positive mindset! Lucky and successful (i.e. optimistic) people believe that everything happens *for* them. They have what is called 'pronoia', or the reverse of paranoia, where they believe that everything happens for their good and in their favour, and that the Universe is conspiring for their good always! It is an extremely fun, uplifting and happy way to live! Remember that everything is available to you. If you think thoughts of victimhood or negativity, you will see things through that lens and/or attract negative things back. Positivity though, is an equal and available choice! The Universe will support you whichever you choose and because positivity is so strong, when you choose the bright side you will receive it back ten times over!

Do not resist challenges because they are opportunities to grow. There is a great opportunity and reason in every challenge. If we see the opportunity and benevolence in change, then our positive attitude has the power to transform our entire world! Pain is momentary and a natural, normal initial reaction to unwanted events – challenges tend to be unexpected and occur when you least expect them! However, the prolonging of suffering is due to our continual, reactionary thoughts to the situation. Change the thoughts, and the feelings must change.

~.Everything Happens for a Reason.~

We tend to experience our most beautiful and deepest transformations from life's most challenging experiences! The thirteenth-century Sufi poet Rumi said: 'The wound is the place where the light enters you.' When we are broken down, or our lives fall apart, it is then that we evolve into the more beautiful, stronger, wiser and more profound version of ourselves! Through challenges, we transform and become more of

Paradise Is a State of Mind

who we really are. Like the beautiful strong wings of a butterfly created through the struggle it faces within its chrysalis, or the pure, indestructible arctic beauty of a diamond formed by eons of pressure, we are formed and shaped into our most powerful, beautiful, creative, wisest and most loving Selves!

The entirety of the Universe is constantly moving you towards your Higher Good and greatest potential – which includes deeper Love. We are born from love, created by Love and we *are* Love. Love is our true nature! The whole purpose of life is to be love, to give love and receive it back to you. It is an infinite, harmonious cycle. The Universe is Love, and through our participation of being love and giving love, we receive it back and it moves through us. The Flow is never-ending. Through our challenges, we are made stronger, wiser and more resilient, and we are also cracked open to allow more Light and Love in! A broken heart is an open heart, and I believe that the heart breaks to open to more and more Love. When I look back on the times in my life I have been hurt the most, the worst heartbreaks were the catalysts to my next best and more loving Self! Heartbreak, grief and hurt are not designed to make you cold, hard and closed off to love! Rather, I believe heartbreak happens for a reason. It is how we think about it that causes the suffering. Even a situation as heartbreaking and challenging as death can be thought of differently; and

-IF YOU BELIEVE IN YOURSELF, ANYTHING IS POSSIBLE-

it seems that in our culture there is a lot of negative thinking around this rite of passage. Everybody and everything dies – even stars. The Sun will eventually die. What is often forgotten or not focused upon is the eternity of Life and Love. Love is eternal. It is never-ending, and although forms change; such is the nature of life, the energy and essence cannot be destroyed and therefore merely changes form.

It is our destiny to become stronger, wiser, more beautiful and profound but also more loving, pure, innocent and full of Love. It may seem paradoxical, yet Life is fundamentally composed of coexisting and harmonizing opposites. As we grow wiser and more aware, we also become more one with our true essence, Love. Love is open-hearted, simple, free and understanding. Love is eternal, a creative primordial Force. It is pure being – Isness. Love is our true nature and our soul's path and yearning is to return home.

Everything in nature works in cycles. There is light and dark, Sun and Moon, death and birth...Yin and Yang. Even in places where there is minimal seasonality, like equatorial regions, there are still small variants of temperature, rainfall, wet and dry seasons, etc. and the life cycles of plants and animals still exist. There is no place on Earth without balance and contrast; seasons and cycles. This means that where there is pain, there is Light, and where there is death,

Paradise Is a State of Mind

there is new life. Nature sows the seed of new creations from the destruction of the former. For example, there are specific plants that grow after the devastation of a forest fire. These plants are known as pyrophytes and they would not be able to grow if it weren't for the fire! These precious, beautiful new seedlings of life sprouting forth from the charred remains of a forest fire perfectly illustrate the magic and dance that is the creation of life!

Even in the infinity of outer space, the cycles of death and regeneration can be observed playing out. Stars, the sources of all life on our planet, are born within the clouds of dust and gas in outer space: nebulae. When a star eventually dies, in some cases it will go supernova, exploding into interstellar space and scattering its remnants across the universe in a cosmic blaze. The remnants of a supernova form more nebulae, which in turn eventually give birth to new stars, and the cycle continues.

Granted, we could argue that one day the process is destined to end in a dead galaxy. However, what we know about the universe, life and even ourselves is currently incomplete. Just like our knowledge about the human body, mind, and nature here on Earth is constantly changing in light of new discoveries, our knowledge of the cosmos is also subject to change. What we currently know about the universe is

-IF YOU BELIEVE IN YOURSELF, ANYTHING IS POSSIBLE-

relatively primitive. At present, it is actually theorized that dead galaxies themselves recycle in another form – that the gas escaping from a dying galaxy settles into the intergalactic and circumgalactic media, later to be condensed into different galaxies! If this theory proves to be correct, which I think it will, it'll just further demonstrate the infinity of our cosmos.

The Universe is constantly expanding. The seasons, cycles and rhythms of nature are constantly reoccurring within the expansion, and I believe that on a grander cosmic scale, everything is expanding within healing spirals of Consciousness. What this means is that the universe – and we as individuals and as a unit – are becoming more healed, purer and greater, deeper Love.

Each new layer of healing that arises moves the trajectory of Love upwards on the whole. The universe is made of Love; it is the glue that holds the cosmos together. Fear exists, but it is merely an illusion. Love is the fundamental Truth of the universe. As the universe constantly expands, Love is constantly expanding. Akin to and equal to the edges of space, Love is ever-expanding and infinite.

We are all individual fragments of a grander Whole; at one with the Universe and all inter-connected with one another. The geometrical fractals found in an individual are miniature representations of the pattern found in the grander Whole. What happens within is also reflected 'out there' as the world is our mirror. As life moves and expands into greater, deeper more primordial layers of Love, this evolution is reflecting in our own inner worlds and vice versa – as we move through deeper layers and levels of our own healing, we contribute to and create the healing and expansion of the universe into more Love.

~.Dark Night of the Soul.~

Even the very worst things that happen to you often turn out to be catalysts for your greater growth! There is a common phenomenon in spirituality called 'dark night of the soul.' I'm sure you have heard of this, and even been through one or two yourself! In the book *Secrets of the Lost Mode of Prayer*, Gregg Braden describes the dark night of the soul as the realization of your worst fear, and this worst fear is unique and specific for everyone. What is highly negative for one person may not seem like a big deal to the next, but that is because we all have our own individual fears. Personally, my worst fear was always to be separated from God. Like everybody, I'd experienced challenges, but I'd always had the strength of my own mind and faith in a Higher

-IF YOU BELIEVE IN YOURSELF, ANYTHING IS POSSIBLE-

Order to things to get through it! Without these things, worldly challenges became a lot harder! As my own mind and connection with the Higher Power was the most important thing for me, it made sense that the worst thing was to be separated from the Universe and Self. What is interesting is that sometimes the dark night of the soul repeats, so the same 'lesson' comes back round but in a different form. For me, I used to experience long-term depression, eventually culminating in some mild hallucinations relating to religion! Funnily enough I was never religious and didn't even believe in God at the time. I remember being so devastated, but after a few months, the natural healing of time (and with it an ushering in of gentler circumstances!) took place and I soon experienced the most profound, beautiful healing and deep transformation! I believe to this day it was Divine intervention, as it began with randomly finding the right mentor and then a series of serendipitous events leading on from that. My first dark night of the soul led to my greatest joy and fulfilment in this life: the discovery of Paradise Consciousness and true Love. Without that dark period beforehand, I don't think the capacity for Paradise in my mind would have existed to that extent!

Coming back to the idea that sometimes the same lesson repeats as another dark night of the soul... I believe that if you go through another dark night of the

Paradise Is a State of Mind

soul with the same or very similar lessons, it is because you are going through a deeper stratum and layer of healing – which means that on the other side lies in wait an even more next-level, deep healing and beautiful transformation!

It is near-impossible to see whilst it is happening, but afterwards when you emerge from these intense situations where you have suffered a lot, you look back and see that every time you were broken down, what arose from the ashes was something three times more beautiful, loving and freer than before! If you look back at your own past dark nights of the soul, can you spot the immense gifts and blessings that emerged from the ruins, and the ways in which you transformed and evolved!? It seems to me that we undergo extreme contrast beforehand to give birth to beautiful, new, profound transformations of our own inner Spirit and Light! Every time we are spiritually 'destroyed', we come out the other end of the tunnel remarkably more beautiful, stronger and transcendent! Like the butterfly emerging from the cocoon with its beautiful strong new wings, we are transformed into our Higher Selves. Best of all, every time you go through this experience, you are also brought much closer to and at one with your Higher Power and your original, true primordial essence of Love.

-IF YOU BELIEVE IN YOURSELF, ANYTHING IS POSSIBLE-

~. The Void

Thankfully, not all challenges are anywhere near as intense as dark nights of the soul! To be fair, dark nights are relatively rare and spaced out throughout our lifetimes and although they lead to the most beautiful new beginnings and transformations, most people don't want to go through them constantly! Life is primarily for joy. There are many smaller challenges throughout our lives, and I wanted to talk about another phenomenon that happens during the transition from the old to the new.

There is an area of inbetween-ness that exists between leaving an old situation and entering the new. You may have been kicked out of your present situation, or something or someone was taken from you and the new hasn't arrived yet – there is just darkness. Not even a sign of the new exists! In that moment, there seems to be only nothing; darkness and emptiness. The Void seems empty, but it is actually teeming with the seeds of new creation. The Void is a space of pure Potentiality, Infinity and New. Within The Void lies infinite possibilities, pure potential and new experiences waiting to be born, to spring into life! Within the darkness lies everything pure, new and innocent. Life is eternal. If life brings you back to zero, remember that zero and Infinity are one. In this

Paradise Is a State of Mind

nothingness and emptiness, there is only pure faith that the next phase of life will emerge. My friend Hollie once likened it to a flying trapeze artist, where the artist must release their first trapeze in order to catch the new! During that time of letting go, there is a space in-between where the artist is temporarily suspended in mid-air with nothing to support them, nothing beneath them... just empty space. During the suspension, all the artist has is pure faith that their partner (the Universe) and the next trapeze (tangible next life circumstance) will emerge from the darkness to catch them.

~.Burnout.~

When we are truly burnt out, we cannot do much for ourselves or see our own way forward. This is the perfect precondition for Divine intervention or a life-transforming miracle to come through, and often happens after a dark night of the soul. It is a state of pure Surrender, birthed from (spiritual) exhaustion and is beautiful.

There is no waste in the universe. Even during times where it looks like there is no point to the length of an extended period of burnout, or it seems like you haven't grown much at all, there is always something deeper

-IF YOU BELIEVE IN YOURSELF, ANYTHING IS POSSIBLE-

happening beneath the surface. The times where you think you aren't growing or haven't done very much at all are actually some of the times where you grow the most! If you have ever gone to the gym or lifted weights, you will know that you make enormous strength gains and improvements during the resting/recovery phases between workouts. Similarly, if you have ever done a sport like gymnastics, you may have had the experience of having months or even years off at a time, and found that when you go back to the activity, after the initial clumsiness of the re-breaking in period, you find that you're stronger and even more competent than ever before! I believe everything happens for a reason, and our down-time is divinely arranged to let our deeper growth take place.

~.Self-Belief.~

Believe in yourself. Encourage yourself and be your own best friend and cheerleader. It is important to treat yourself with the utmost care, respect and compassion always. This is a delicate yet resilient time of new beginnings, healing, growth and increase. The new sprouts into life simultaneously and alongside the dying of the old, and so growth and progress are not linear. This is why sometimes it looks like one step

Paradise Is a State of Mind

forward, two steps back... yet all the time we are growing and moving upwards to the sun!

Trust in the process of Life and always believe in *yourself*. Self-belief, resilience and optimism are amongst the most powerful gifts we have! Believing in yourself and your own inevitable success will encourage you to try new things, take new risks and carry on moving forward – to even bigger and better things. Not only is it remarkably brave to be open, vulnerable and willing to try again after 'failure' or loss, it is actually more effacing. We require optimism and self-belief to move forward and try again after we are hurt or lost! We are naturally hard-wired towards resilience and success. The time-honoured example of a baby getting up to walk, refusing to judge or criticize itself after its previous failure, is a classic for a reason! That baby gets to places!

My friend Ryan once told me that the most successful people in life fail a lot more times than ordinary people do.

At our core, we are incredibly strong, brave, gifted, talented and courageous. Our spirits are of Fire. It takes remarkable strength, bravery and self-belief to face the challenges Life lovingly places before us, because as humans we will always have fears and doubts. It's unrealistic to expect to never get upset or

-IF YOU BELIEVE IN YOURSELF, ANYTHING IS POSSIBLE-

frightened by challenges, no matter how many times you've been through them and succeeded! We will always have our human vulnerability. In challenging times, it is best to soothe yourself however best you can and go within and listen to your inner voice. Our intuition is our best guide to lead us through life's storms. When we listen to our own inner voice and trust the innate Goodness and the process of Life, we have a smoother and easier time navigating through challenges.

Everything that is lost is found again, and everything that is hurt is healed again. Within every major life challenge or obstacle that comes your way, a massive opportunity lies in wait ahead. All events work out beautifully, magically and serendipitously for you in the end. As my dear friend Andreja says, 'Everything will be okay in the end, and if it's not okay, it's not the end.'

Paradise Is a State of Mind

~SELF-BELIEF AFFIRMATIONS~

- Everything happens for my Highest Good. Life is always moving towards my greatest growth and deepest potential. My life is always moving into higher and deeper levels of Love.

- Everything happens for me. Miracles and blessings lie in wait around the corner from every challenge. My life is blessed, divinely led and protected.

- Everything is unfolding perfectly. Everything is unfolding in accordance to a Higher Plan.

- Everything happens for a reason. I am always divinely taken care of. I am always in the divine right place at the divine right time.

- I admire my bravery and I love, honour and cherish myself! I encourage and believe in myself.

- When you believe in yourself, anything is possible.

-IF YOU BELIEVE IN YOURSELF, ANYTHING IS POSSIBLE-

- I am my own best friend and my own best cheerleader always. The Universe and I believe in me.

- I am divinely guided, protected and watched over. Everything is happening right on time. I am exactly where I need to be.

- I am always divinely directed to arrive at the perfect place at the perfect time.

- Life loves me. Everything is unfolding perfectly for me. I trust Destiny.

- I am ever-safe in the universe. Life loves me.

- I am wrapped in a cocoon of divine safety and protection. I am so deeply loved by the Universe!

- I am one with the Power that created me.

- Life is primordially good. The Universe is primordial Good, and loving. I am constantly loved, blessed and watched over.

Paradise Is a State of Mind

- Life is working out for me in ways I can't even dream of yet.

- Everything leads me to the right place, at the perfect time.

- Life is not merely a series of meaningless accidents or coincidences, but rather it's a tapestry of events that culminate in an exquisite, sublime plan.

- Everything is leading me here, to this place, to this moment.

- Things magically and beautifully work out for me in the most serendipitous and wondrous ways.

- There is a Divine plan.

- I trust Life.

- I love life. I am so grateful to be alive!

-IF YOU BELIEVE IN YOURSELF, ANYTHING IS POSSIBLE-

- I embrace and welcome challenges. Challenges make me stronger. Challenges transform me into the next best version of my Self.

- Every experience is a hidden opportunity/blessing in disguise for me to become more of who I am. Every experience shapes me into my Higher Self.

- Life loves me and is there for me always!

- All of my dreams come true in the perfect time-space sequence. Everything is intricately and seamlessly connected.

- There is a Divine Order and Flow to life.

- I embrace and welcome the Flow of Life. I envelope myself in the mystery and the beauty of the unknown.

- Within darkness and Void, lies infinite possibilities and potential. What is coming is always better than what is gone.

Paradise Is a State of Mind

- Everything happens for a reason. Everything happens to bless me.

- Life works for my good and in my favour always.

- There is a magic, beauty and serendipity to Life! I welcome the Unknown. Within uncertainty, lies challenge and excitement.

- Powerful transformations and beautiful new beginnings are seedlings within the ashes of every destruction. I trust and celebrate the cycles of Life!

- There is untold Good in the Universe. The Universe is nothing but Love and Good. Everything is *for* me.

- I am always moving into my Greater Good.

- Life is always there for me. I embrace the power of endings and new beginnings!

- Miracle after miracle pops into my reality.

-IF YOU BELIEVE IN YOURSELF, ANYTHING IS POSSIBLE-

- New Good flows to me in a river of Love and wonder.

- I live in a beautiful, miraculous universe. Miracles are normal for me.

- I live in a universe of Love and miracles.

- Love and Good are my reality. Paradise is my reality.

Paradise Is a State of Mind

8.

-GOALS, AMBITIONS AND DREAMS-

I believe that each deep and true dream of our heart and soul has been planted there by Destiny and is meant for us. The realization may not always look exactly how we expect when it does realize, but if so then it will always be better and far beyond what you asked for, because the Universe constantly works towards our Higher Good!! We are always receiving what is for our Highest evolution, whether we like it or not! We never need to really worry about where our life is going, because we are always being taken to what's best for us, and far beyond our limited human imagination. Our conscious thinking is very limited compared to the Divine Mind, and so what we think we want is usually only the very beginning for what our soul has planned for us!!

-GOALS, AMBITIONS AND DREAMS-

We want our dreams because of the promise of emotional fulfilment they carry! If you fill yourself with the feelings of fulfilment, love, gratitude, joy and excitement (i.e. satisfaction) first, then your dreams, when they do manifest, will be fulfilling and carry these same energies!! We colour the frequencies of our feelings into our world around us; and so when you become and radiate love, joy and gratitude, you summon these energies back to you in like form! This way, you'll never need to worry about whether or not your dreams will be fulfilling, or if they'll be not what you expected or disappointing, because as you emit gratitude and fulfilment *first*, the outside always mirrors the inside. You feel the frequency of fulfilment first by realizing you already have everything you ever wanted or needed right here and now – because you are one with your Higher Power. You are one with a limitless, loving, supernatural Power who adores you and is at one with you, and who loved you enough to make you aware of itself and your own power to create! The thoughts you think paint your reality, and you can think anything you want. Your power to create Paradise in your life is truly limitless. You are free already, because you have the power of your mind and it is only truly you and the Power that created you in

Paradise Is a State of Mind

your universe.

The Universe is *for* you having your dreams, because it is a creative Power! You have been given the power to create to use for something; to shape and make forms and to artistically express yourself!! You are the painter of your own life, and your words, thoughts and actions are the tools you use to create the beautiful, dreamlike canvas of your life.

If you dream about what you want, I think it is best to always dream really big. The only thing that limits us is ourselves, and so if we set extraordinary goals for ourselves, we tend to achieve them. The Universe will always give you back ten times over what you asked for, because Love is generous, lavish and limitless. When you give out Love, it tends to come back ten times over! Love endlessly multiplies and generates more of itself. The more Love you give out, the more Love grows, multiplies and comes back to you. The Energy of Love itself is very loving, because it only ever creates more of itself, between people and out in the universe.

When you set extraordinary goals out of Love, their realization tends to benefit everyone else involved. It is

-GOALS, AMBITIONS AND DREAMS-

like magic. The people involved in making your dream come true will also somehow greatly benefit from you realizing your dreams! You will realize it when you see it in action. For example, when you acquire your dream job, your customers will benefit, your boss, and everyone else you also meet through working there! Even if *you* are the one directly receiving tips and bonuses, etc., the value you give to your customers, boss, acquaintances, etc., will be worth 2-3 times more than what you receive. Your happiness benefits others so much more than you realize! I believe this works vibrationally, as when you are happy and your heart is being fulfilled, you emit transcendent, Love-based, high-vibrational energy that is naturally good for all!! This pure, positive loving energy has a rich, knock-on dominos effect on the world around you and at large.

This fulfilment and joy energy also works on another level: the Divine Intelligence of the Universe is the ultimate Master Planner, and is mind-blowingly skilled at bringing people together in a mutually beneficial Higher Plan!! In the vibrational field of Love, everybody wins. Love and transcendence are win-win energies. Everybody wins in the game of Love.

When you do set your goals, and dream as big as you

Paradise Is a State of Mind

want: script or write out how you will feel, and really allow yourself to enjoy these feelings! Bring them into your body and saturate in them for several minutes! I usually do this by writing the same thing over and over again until it feels like enough, or until I feel 'full.' This brief scripting I feel is enough, and then you can just get on with your day, trusting that any action steps you will need to take will be delivered to you in Divine Timing!! Inspired action will always be delivered to you as and when you need it. All you need to do is just live your life as your dreams unfold. The potency of the energy you've created is so strong, and your dream is working on your behalf! As you go about your day, taking care of your daily business and enjoying your life, your dreams are working tirelessly behind the scenes to realize themselves. The Divine Mind will give you prompts of what to do next; where you need to go, what you need to do, at the perfect time. Let it Flow!

When you do receive the realization of your dream, it will probably just be randomly in the course of your life! You don't need to watch or wait on tenterhooks; it is best to just get on with your life, knowing that you've done your best to put your goal out there, and are taking the action steps as and when needed! This doesn't mean to do nothing unless it's blatantly

-GOALS, AMBITIONS AND DREAMS-

inspired. 'Inspired action' isn't always obvious, and often your manifestation will come from action that felt so ordinary/natural, you won't even realize it was inspired until retrospect! The best thing to do is to just live your life as fully and joyously as you can – which includes taking any actions that arise that feel fun, curious, exciting or even just having the potential to lead you to your dreams! We never really know how anything will happen. That is what life is all about... the mystery, excitement and the adventure of the unknown! The mystery and unknowingness of the process of Life is what makes it so wondrous and eventful!

Make yourself as happy as possible in this time. Do the things you love, try new things, go to new places, meet new people and spend time with the people you love! Similar to what author Louise Hay says in her book *I Can Do It*, tend to your soil and fertilize it with joy, love and positivity! One day, in Divine Timing, the flower will bloom and the seed was sprouting all along. Life loves you, and wants to prosper you. It wants your dreams to come true because joy, satisfaction/excitement and fulfilment are the meaning of life. Tend to your soil, fertilizing it with love, joy and

Paradise Is a State of Mind

happiness, and your plants will grow with vibrant, alive green energy, tall and strong with solid foundational roots!

The garden analogy for manifestation is one of the best analogies ever made I think. I don't know if [Louise Hay] invented it, but it demonstrates the value of patience, trust, Divine Timing and the co-creative process.

Give out love, joy and fulfilment in your daily life as much as you can, without waiting on your goals, because you don't need them! Remember that everything you need is inside you now. You have a silent, Divine co-creative partner who is working with your soul to fulfil the Grand Plan of your life. Remember, your desires have been planted in your heart by the Divine because they are its plan for you as a unique expression of itself. Your desires are Life's plan to express itself through you, so in a way it is a selfish thing as Universe is using you to fulfil its own plans. Propitiously, what Life wants for itself is also a direct match to what you want, because your ideas are a mirror of the Divine Mind! So, you never need to worry about your goals, and you can relax. Life will move Heaven and Earth to bring your dreams into reality as

-GOALS, AMBITIONS AND DREAMS-

you show up to life, and give you every nudge and prompt you need for you to take the perfect right action step at the divine time.

Take care of your love, joy and gratitude in the now. Taking care of your love, joy and happiness in the now guarantees that the seeds you sow in the present will continue to reap love, joy and harmony in the future. Paradise is here and now. You get what you give. As you emit love, joy and gratitude in the now, Paradise manifests all around you, now and forever. There is no time; so whatever you are giving out now is coming back to you in like form.

Paradise Is a State of Mind

~•DREAM LIFE AFFIRMATIONS•~

- I am living the life of my dreams.

- My dream life has materialized now, and I am so incredibly, blissfully happy.

- I have everything I ever wanted or needed.

- Everything I desire, I receive. My needs and desires are met before I even ask.

- I love life. How incredible it is to be alive!

- Every day is a blessing, a gift, a quiet joy and Paradise. I am always in the Present moment.

- I love life and am glad to be alive!! Every day I radiate joy as I dwell on and luxuriate in how blessed I am!!

-GOALS, AMBITIONS AND DREAMS-

- I love myself and the Power that created me. I am one with the Universe. It is only me and my Higher Power in my world. I am safe.

- Life is infinitely and boundlessly loving, purely paradisiacal, benevolent, and only ever concerned with my Good. Life loves me so much, beyond the stars. There is no limit to the Universe's incredible love for me.

- I am deeply, *deeply* loved by this boundless Universe. The reaches of Life's love for me insurmountably pass time and space.

- Since the beginning of time, I am deeply, infinitely loved by Source. I was created in Love, I *am* Love and I am surrounded by Love always.

- Every day I wake up rejoicing in how blessed I am!! I feel so good, and am so safe.

- Life loves me. Life wants nothing but good for me!

- I am so blessed by the Universe. My entire life is magical.

Paradise Is a State of Mind

- I am always in the Flow. Life loves me. The Universe's incredible love for me knows no bounds.

- I radiate joy, love and incredible fulfilment out into the world; beyond space, time and infinity. I am at the heart of the Universe; at the heart of Creation. I am at the centre of Love.

- I am one with Life: one with incredible love, passion, joy and endless gratitude.

- Bliss is my nature. Truth is my nature. I bring love wherever I go.

- My life is a pure living Paradise; Heaven on Earth.

- I am *deeply* fulfilled living the life of my dreams.

- I am the heart of the Universe.

- I radiate Love, passion and Creation. Everything I desire, I receive.

- I am one with the Universe.

-GOALS, AMBITIONS AND DREAMS-

Paradise Is a State of Mind

9.

-SOULMATES-

*T*his chapter is for finding the love of your life – your one and only True Love soulmate! I believe that soulmates are out there for each and every one of us, and they are perfect for us. Each person has someone out there who is everything they want and more, who feels the exact same way about them and with whom the relationship is Paradise!

When you find Love within yourself, you naturally exude Love out to others and it comes back to you multiplied. Love is infinite, never-ending and ever-creative. When you give out Love, it only ever creates more of itself and comes back to you in like form, as more Love. One of the strongest forms of Love that can manifest in a person's life is a True Love soulmate, because for most people this type of connection feels like Heaven on Earth.

You are one with the Power that runs the entire universe, and the Power that created you is also within you. You are always safe. It is helpful, joyous and

113

-SOULMATES-

freeing to know that this Power also gave you the power to create. You can never truly lack love or have it come from outside of you, because everyone is just a reflection of the Love you carry within you. People are really just mirrors of us, and so as we attune to the energy of Source Love, we attract to us magnetically and ten times over people who are on that same frequency, and who have the same feelings as us!! This is our soul family: our soul friends, soul colleagues, clients and of course our soulmates. When you know that you are the Source of Love, because you are one with the Power within and you already have everything inside of you, you can never feel lonely. Life is here for you and the love you seek is within you.

When you are full of Source Energy, Love and Paradise, because Source Energy wants to create more of itself, you will probably be inspired to create an intention: to verbalize or put down on paper everything that you want and the type of person you're looking for! If you have never had the idea or desire for your Heaven on Earth soulmate before, they might not materialize in your life straight away, but the idea of them will come. Once you set your intention, you are magnetic to it!! Love is such a powerful, strong, magnetic and transcendent energy that it draws everything in is likeness to it. You will be led to the perfect people, places, circumstances and events you need to meet your One, or they will find you right where you are! You

Paradise Is a State of Mind

don't even need to plan about how you could possibly meet someone, or dream of ways to make it happen! The way will come to you.

Dream big when it comes to manifesting your soulmate, because you really can have anything you want! If you desire your soulmate, then he or she is meant for you. There is a perfect person out there for everyone. Do not feel that you are asking for too much, if you want someone who is perfect in your eyes. There truly is someone out there for everyone, and I believe that the people who are meant for us (not just soulmates but also soul friends, soul colleagues, etc.) are designed exactly the way they are, in order to fit with the people who are also meant for them!! Meaning, that if you think someone is perfect or amazing, they will also be thinking this about you. You are attracted to these people because they are your people. When you go for who you're drawn to in life, everybody wins. The spirit of Love arranges divine encounters for the Highest Good of all concerned. There are no mistakes in this universe. It is all a perfect, Divine, Higher Intelligent Design, interlaced and woven with Divine Love and Harmony. The perfect person you find attractive will be absolutely crazy about you back, and they will think that *you* are the most beautiful thing they've ever seen!

We truly do live in a limitless universe, and the Universe can and does create things – including people

-SOULMATES-

– out of thin air! Or at least that is what it will seem like. The Universe has a way of bringing people together who are so perfect for one another that it will seem like the other person really was created out of thin air. It is uncanny the way the right person fits what you want so perfectly. Dream very big when it comes to your soulmate... it really is one of the most important things, so when it comes to this one heart's desire, always be true to yourself in your asking.

The most time-honoured and traditional advice of writing a soulmate list and making a vision board is something I highly recommend! Not only is it extremely fun, but also when your soulmate actually appears in your reality, you will be thrilled and delighted as you look back at your vision board/list, and see all the things that came true – even the minutest details like the T-shirt someone was wearing on an image on your vision board, or you may even manifest someone with the exact same full name!! The Universe really does love to draw upon the ethers of our imagination when painting our dreams upon the canvas of our reality!!

I would never advise trying to manifest someone specific (including celebrities) when manifesting a soulmate. Because the Universe is limitless, you really wouldn't want to chase after a specific person or put

Paradise Is a State of Mind

anyone else on a pedestal; it makes the power balance unequal and puts you in a 'chaser' dynamic in my opinion, even if it's only energetically. When you are very confident in yourself and realize how beautiful, worthy and special you are, you won't feel the need or desire to manifest anybody specific, including celebrities! It may be fun to do so, but this kind of thing is really nothing compared to the deep, true bond of long-lasting soulmate love, which has been arranged by the Universe and created within the Heart space! When you are very high-vibrational, you will be less and less attached to specific people, places, circumstances and events anyway. You can still love and enjoy specific things/people/circumstances/events, but at the same time you will feel a healthy non-attachment to them, because as you are deeply connected to Source, you know instinctually that Source is your only true wellspring of Love and Creation!! You know that you will never need to be attached to any specific person, circumstance, event or job, because Source is truly limitless, and if something doesn't work out, then there is always something bigger and better around the corner.

That does not mean that you should be disloyal or keep your options open when you are with your soulmate! I

117

-SOULMATES-

personally subscribe to 120% loyalty and faithfulness, and I will lose all real interest and attraction to anybody else when I'm truly in love with someone. I would expect a guy to be the same with me. Ignore all myths about 'all people being the same' or your dreams being impossible; e.g. 'all women want rich, successful smart men, all women are interested in alpha male types, all men are disloyal and unfaithful, all men always keep their eyes open in a relationship,' etc. These are all complete and utter rubbish! It may appear true at the ego-level, which forms the world of illusion (where a lot of people dwell when they are in a low-vibration). However, we are not living in the world of illusion! We are living – and aiming to live as full-time as possible – in the High-Vibrational, transcendent world created by Love, Joy, Gratitude, and all those other positive high-vibrational emotions! The world that these positive thoughts and energies create is a very different, *paradisiacal* reality – one of Love, trust, mutual understanding, safety, security, bliss, mutual fulfilment and Oneness!

Your soulmate will be completely, breathtakingly, transcendently beautiful/handsome and attractive to you. You will find them deeply fulfilling, exciting and thrilling, and yet you will feel completely safe with them and at peace at the same time. They will be crazy about you, be everything you ever wanted and more, and they will love you back just as much as you love

Paradise Is a State of Mind

them, if not just a tiny bit *more*. They will be forever, deeply head-over-heels in love with you. Your soulmate will be loyal, devoted to you and voluntarily faithful because they want to be, because the thought of others will make them feel sick and upset! They will think that *you* are the most beautiful/handsome/gorgeous person they've ever seen. You will take their breath away. They will be excited and nervous around you, and get butterflies around you. They will always be day-dreaming of a life and a future with you.

Your soulmate will always be there for you, even at your worst because soulmate love is pure and unconditional. You are already perfect in your soulmate's eyes. Even at your worst, they will think that you are beautiful , unique and special. Your soulmate will stay by your side during the best times and the worst, because they see you as perfect and worth the effort. Soulmate love is loyal, forever, devoted, permanent, durable, forgiving, graceful and understanding, and carries all the qualities of Source Love. A soulmate is generally the strongest reflection of Source Love that can appear in your life, and so it naturally carries the same qualities of the love that Source has for you.

You will never want anybody else or get bored of your soulmate. They will completely and deeply fulfil you

119

-SOULMATES-

on every level, and it is a forever love! A soulmate relationship will only ever get better, deeper and *more*. They will usually also improve your life, and help you to grow in ways that you couldn't when you were single. Together as a couple, you will accelerate each other's financial and career success, and grow in other ways you never foresaw when you were single! I believe that this happens because happiness (joy and fulfilment) promotes success and growth. The high vibrations and pure Source Love that a soulmate brings into your life uplifts and overspills into all other areas of life!! You may also find your friendships, health and any other life areas improving too.

Usually, your soulmate will also make you laugh, and you will find them very funny and hilarious, because fun and joy are high vibrations and qualities of Source Love!! One of the highest-vibrational aspects of Source Love is light-heartedness, fun and joy!

You don't even have to search for your soulmate – as soon as you set your intention to be with them, it will start happening! Love vibration is *so* magnetic, that as you fill yourself up with Love (by connecting to Source), you will become powerfully magnetic to your dreams and desires right where you are – including your soulmate! You won't have to do anything outside of your normal daily life, unless of course you feel the urge or inspiration to go somewhere or do something

Paradise Is a State of Mind

different! If you do feel that urge or inspiration, then of course follow it! Often, your soulmate might be in another place if you are an extraordinary dreamer, or like travelling or adventure. If you are one of those people who are meant to meet your One in another place, then the Universe will move Heaven and Earth to get you to the divine right place in the divine right time! Follow the impulses of the Universe.

You can be brought together with your soulmate in a way that makes you happy, and fulfils you! For example, if you dislike using dating apps or websites, then please don't use them! Personally, I don't! I'm well aware that most people use them nowadays, and that it's 'normal' to meet the One online, but for me I know that this will never be my way personally, so I don't bother wasting my energy. What you believe comes true for you. What you give out, is what you get back! If you truly believe that you can meet someone in a natural, organic and serendipitous way, then that reality becomes available to you. You can easily meet people at work, a grocery store, at a cafe, a bar, at a party, or perhaps a neighbour from your apartment block! The Universe has zero problem bringing people together naturally. It has been done that way for millions of years before the twenty-first century.

You can also use affirmations such as: 'I am a magnet for serendipity/romance and divine chance encounters wherever I go!' or 'I am a magnet for love/an Eros/Aphrodite!' You could even meet the love of your life on the street! There are countless options. I'm sure at some point you have crushed on or even given your number to a cute bartender or grocery store clerk! These are just some small examples of the myriad of ways for meeting your soulmate. Affirm: 'I am open and magnetic to love wherever I go', or 'I am so lucky in love!' 'I constantly attract/magnetize the *best* people I like wherever I go.' Be open and available for the reality where you meet people in spontaneous and serendipitous ways, and this is what you'll create! You are the Creator of your life, and Life will give you back what you give it.

Intuition is also a powerful thing when finding your soulmate. Your intuition is extremely heightened when you're at the Love level. When you manifest your soulmate, you are normally predominantly residing at Love vibration, so it makes sense that sharp intuition comes with finding the One. A lot of the time, when you're at Love vibration, your discernment is extremely high, and so you can instinctively sense whenever something isn't right, and quickly end things so you're free to move on!

Sometimes however, there may be a period of uncertainty when you meet someone (especially if that person is a 95% match to what you want, but there is a

Paradise Is a State of Mind

glaring 5% missing!) and so you just have to ride it out and see where it goes. Time will tell if someone is your One or not. Either the connection will reach a natural endpoint or conclusion, or you will work out your issues together and heal, dissolving any old wounds and transcending karma together faster!

If things do end with the person you thought was the One, then know that even though ultimately they didn't turn out to be your true soulmate, you are still very close! If you were 95-100% convinced that someone was your soulmate, and it ended, then this is still fantastic news. It just means that what you asked for is right around the corner. If there was just 5% or less missing from your demonstration, then your vibration has progressed tremendously towards what you want. Remember, eyes on the prize (from Chapter 6). Do not be deterred by any illusions that don't work out. Keep your eyes fixed on your destination, and keep moving. Your soulmate will be here before you even turn the corner.

There is a reason for these types of hurtful experiences. It is usually that you have some last residual healing to do before you are truly ready for your soulmate. These 95%/'almost'-matches will polish you off and refine you, like a diamond crafted to dazzling perfection by the tools used for its brillianteering!

-SOULMATES-

In the second, less common scenario where it really does end up working out with the person you were unsure about, then that time of anxiety and uncertainty was also for a reason. It will somehow serve the both of you in the long run, healing parts of you that needed to be healed before you were brought together forever, and making you mature and available to be the best partners to each other when you are in your solid future relationship.

If something really is clearly no longer working out, then you know that it's safe to release this person, and let go and release *yourself* to your Highest Good!! In these scenarios, someone even **better** is waiting for you! This is true even if you can't envision it right now! The Universe is infinite, limitless, and has zero problem creating and bringing you together with someone way better. We are the ones who can sometimes block or temporarily delay our manifestation by saying things like: 'there couldn't possibly be anyone better... he/she was perfect. They were definitely my One. They fitted 95-99% of my soulmate list.' This may have been true at first, but if the relationship has progressed to the point where you are left sad and heartbroken, then it is in your best interests to let go!! If they really are the One, then you'll be brought back together naturally anyway, and the Universe will work it out. Letting go of this person won't change that. When something is truly meant to be – especially soulmates – the Universe

Paradise Is a State of Mind

moves Heaven and Earth to make sure those two people end up together at the perfect time. Nothing you can do will stop that, including letting go! And, if he or she really wasn't the right one, then releasing them opens you up to the energies of Trust, optimism and faith!! Faith, confidence and self-belief are extremely magnetizing, attractive and pull your Good in towards you much faster! Fear, worry and doubt are weak and repellent energies that can temporarily delay or keep out your Good. However, when you unwaveringly choose faith, determined self-belief and optimism, knowing that you *do* get what you want, it pulls your Good in towards you (your real soulmate) that much faster!!

Claim for yourself: 'My true soulmate is out there, and he or she is so much *better* than the person I'm releasing now! He or she is even *more* attractive, even more exciting, thrilling and fulfilling to me, even *more* into me, and they are so much nicer, kinder, thoughtful and _____ (any other quality you deem vital in your soulmate!) He/she treats me *so* much better, and the relationship Flows! It is a Divine, Heaven on Earth union. This union is divinely blessed. My new/true person loves me and wants me so much, and I feel even more Bliss and Paradise with them!! It is true Heaven on Earth, and deeply, 120% fulfilling on every level. I feel so safe, confident, loved and attractive with them!! Thank you Universe for my perfect, divine love of dreams. I am one with Life.' Use the power of your positive affirmations to create.

You will be completely in awe and gratitude of how perfect your soulmate is! You will be deeply, mutually fulfilled by him/her, and in awe of how they match your unique preferences down to an eerie tee! They will be the absolute epitome of perfection, excitement and fulfilment to you, and they will feel exactly the same way about you as you do about them, if not even *more*. They will leave you breathtaken, be the most beautiful person you've ever seen (or one of them), and they will be even *more* loving, attentive, loyal, and whatever other qualities you need, than anyone you've ever met up until now! They will be everything you ever dreamed of and more.

When you are living at the Love level, the Universe grants and fulfils your desires and dreams even more extremely, extravagantly and abundantly than before. Love delivers results above and beyond, and at this high-vibrational level, it tends to be permanent.

Paradise Is a State of Mind

~·LOVE AFFIRMATIONS·~

- I am now together with my soulmate, and it is Heaven on Earth.

- I am now together with my soulmate, and it is everything I asked for and more.

- I *deeply* love my soulmate, and my soulmate loves me just as much back as I love them, if not even more.

- I am so blissfully happy with my soulmate! Life with my soulmate is Heaven on Earth.

- This union is divinely blessed. It's Heaven on Earth! The Universe has brought us together.

- I love *everything* about my soulmate. He/she/they are perfect in my eyes!

-SOULMATES-

- My soulmate is breathtakingly handsome/beautiful and good-looking/attractive! My soulmate takes my breath away.

- My soulmate leaves me weak at the knees and leaves me walking on air. He/she leaves me breathless.

- My soulmate treats me like a King/Queen/Princess/Prince/Goddess/Knight/Angel.

- My soulmate constantly pursues me. My soulmate always moves our courtship forwards.

- I have *no* doubts about my soulmate's feelings for me. It's so obvious!

- I feel so loved, safe and truly secure and at peace with my soulmate. He/she makes me feel confident, beautiful, gorgeous and perfect.

- I am deeply, 120% fulfilled on every level with my soulmate. They take my breath away and leave me in awe. I never want anybody else.

Paradise Is a State of Mind

- The relationship only ever gets better and better, and *more*.

- I feel so safe with my soulmate. He/she is there for me unconditionally with unwavering support. He/she still loves me at my absolute worst. I am perfect in their eyes.

- My soulmate allows me to love and be there for him/her in hard times. Our relationship is mutually supportive, loving and nurturing.

- Soulmate love is unconditional. My soulmate is there for me through the absolute worst times, and allows me to support and be there for them in return. Our relationship is supportive, mutually beneficial, giving, forgiving, permanent and durable.

- I feel so safe being vulnerable, authentic and open with my soulmate. My soulmate truly loves me. They find my vulnerability beautiful. It makes them love me even more.

-SOULMATES-

- My soulmate finds my vulnerability deeply attractive. It makes them even more attracted to me.

- Every time my soulmate and I have an issue, it brings us closer together, strengthens us and heals our wounds.

- My soulmate heals and evolves me in ways that are extremely accelerative for my spiritual growth! They help me to transcend old baggage and karma, and help evolve me to my Highest, most beautiful Self.

- My soulmate cooks for me/adores my cooking. They love setting up a beautiful, idyllic home with me.

- My soulmate wants a dog (or cat) and a family with me. It is their idea.

- My soulmate is constantly daydreaming of marriage, a future, a family and/or a life with me! I am unquestionably the One for them.

Paradise Is a State of Mind

- My soulmate knew I was the One from the very beginning. It was love at first sight for them.

- My soulmate is amazing… I never want anyone else. Sometimes, I can't believe a person so perfect actually exists.

- My soulmate is my love of dreams.

- The connection is lightning, fire, electric and Heaven on Earth.

- Our union is divinely blessed. Everything flows so easily with my soulmate. The Universe and my soulmate do minimum 54% of the work! I relax.

- I feel so safe with my soulmate. My soulmate makes me feel so loved! I am fulfilled on every level.

- This relationship is never-ending Heaven on Earth.

- Life just gets better and better with my soulmate. My soulmate and I live permanent Heaven on

-SOULMATES-

Earth. I am safe in the universe, and Life is ever-loving and eternally fulfilling.

10.

-SACRAL BEAUTY-

*T*his chapter is about feeling beautiful, confident and amazing about yourself! If we ever want to create physical changes in ourselves, it is almost always because really what we want is to feel good about ourselves inside. If you can feel good about yourself first, you will attract all sorts of situations, circumstances, people and events that reflect and mirror your own positive feelings of self-love and self-worth back to you!!

Inner Confidence.~

The feeling of loving yourself, being delighted with who you are and how you look, loving your appearance and rejoicing at your inner qualities are the deepest ways to radiate beauty! When you truly love who you are on a deep level, it makes it pretty easy to love how you look

-SACRAL BEAUTY-

and appreciate and be thankful for your unique beauty. Also, not that it's really important, but if you'd like others to appreciate you more and see your beauty, if you appreciate yourself and how amazing you are *first*, other people will always pick up on it and reflect your own positive feelings of self-worth back to you like a mirror!! We are all made individual and unique and there are dazzlingly beautiful qualities in *everybody*.

A good exercise if you ever have a hard time recognizing your worth is to list out all your accomplishments, all the compliments you've ever received (both on your appearance AND your inner qualities), all the things you love, things that make you *deeply* happy and joyful and also your most treasured moments with your closest friends/family, or just experiences you've had that left you with an incredible feeling! This connects you to the essence of You – you at your most True Self and when you're fully connected to Source. That is the most magnetic and gorgeous expression of you! You cannot be any more beautiful than you are when you're connected to Source and the Oneness of your True Self!!

That doesn't mean you have to force yourself to be happy all the time, and you are still beautiful and lovable even when you're having sad days or hard times! Beauty, flow, receiving and Divine Grace are found in openness, vulnerability, honesty and allowing –

Paradise Is a State of Mind

allowing the flow of your emotions. Honouring all of your emotions and allowing yourself to be sad is one of the deepest ways you can honour yourself and honour the Universe. When we shut off the vulnerable inner child part of ourselves, it shuts down the Universe because the Universe made us human and imperfect in the first place. Paradoxically, there is perfection in imperfection. We accept that life is an ornate tapestry made of the sad times, the joyous times and the outright ecstatic blissful times and Paradise!! But it's the challenges also that provide immense value because they make us who we are; and they always push us and transform us into the highest, most evolved, wisest and beautiful version of ourselves!!

~.Uniqueness.~

My friend Ryan also once told me 'You have to remember as well that everybody has different eyes.' Everybody has a different idea of what they find attractive and beautiful. The 'society ideal' is always changing, and as I write this book in 2023, the Victoria's Secret model slim & athletic physique from 2015 (the year he told me that) has already been replaced by a new trend. It has been this way for centuries, and in another five years, the new trend will be replaced by something else. This is why it is

-SACRAL BEAUTY-

important to love how *you* specifically look and admire and appreciate your own unique self, to the point where you would never want to be anyone else! *You* are your own ideal. **You** are the number one 'idol' in your life.

We all have unique traits, both physically and internally that make us stunningly, eye-catchingly beautiful and, most importantly, heart-capturingly beautiful. Beauty is not about how somebody looks but it is about how someone makes you *feel*. That is why inner beauty is so important and transcendent.

We are all unique, divine creative expressions of Life! When we celebrate the unique gift of who we are, we tap into an energy of gratitude that we have been created with Divine love and careful consideration! I believe we were designed exactly on purpose the way we are for a reason, and a lot of thought has gone into our unique physical traits, characteristics, personalities and individual talents, gifts and interests!! Beauty is an amalgamation of the body, heart, mind, spirit and soul. Our bodies are uniquely designed vessels for our souls that reflect the inner us.

Life loves diversity and uniqueness amongst Creation. Variety, individuality and everyone coexisting harmoniously, perfectly complementing and strengthening each other symbiotically – this is the

Paradise Is a State of Mind

Love and Beauty of the Universe. A mysterious, sleek black panther is just as striking and beautiful as a colourful, showy bird of paradise. A rose is just as ethereally beautiful and visually stunning as a lily. Even plants and animals from the same species are never exactly alike! There are always variations between individuals; for example, in humans identical twins have different fingerprints from one another. In nature, every rock has different texture, form and markings to the others, no tree ever has the exact same twist to its branches or interplay of colours woven amongst its foliage and no snowflake is ever exactly like the one that came before or another one to fall! No sunset will ever be the same as another one that has set the sky extraordinarily on fire. Nature never re-creates anyone or anything exactly the same and therefore each creation is utterly special and unique.

If you have ever felt jealous of another, it's only because you're not feeling fully fulfilled within yourself and your own unique expression of that thing. For example, if you ever felt jealous of someone else's body, it's because you're not feeling that you're fully expressing your own fullest potential when it comes to your body. What you are actually wanting and admiring is the highest and most feel-good version of your own body! This is true for all areas of life – health, career, money, lifestyle and wealth, etc. You never actually want what someone else has but rather you want your own best version of it. So know that if you ever feel jealousy, it's only showing you what you need to work on developing for yourself! Often, especially when it comes to our bodies and how we look, what we actually need to work on for ourselves is our confidence rather than actual physical changes. So many times, we are already gifted with the most incredible and rare beauty and we fail to see it! Everybody has equal beauty and value because we were all created with a purpose. God would not have created different features, skin tones, shapes, sizes, quirks, personality traits, etc. if each one didn't have equal value and merit. As humans, sometimes we create judgements and neglect that everybody has different tastes – that beauty is truly in the eye of the beholder! There is no society ideal that is more powerful than True Beauty – the truth that we are all equally beautiful, worthy and special in our own right. When you know this, it is easy to fully love, accept and embrace the unique gift of who you are! Your own unique, magnetic Self is 1000 times more beautiful, fascinating and interesting than if you were just a carbon copy of somebody else.

There is somebody for everyone. Every person has an ideal that they find the most attractive to *them*. Everybody has a unique set of friends, lovers, soulmate, colleagues, clients, etc. who they find the best and most ideal people for them. I believe that we are all perfectly and deliberately designed exactly how we are in a way that complements what our soul family/people/soulmates also find the most attractive and beautiful. The very features that are the truest essence of You will be the same features that your soulmate and soul people will be crazy about and find most attractive! This applies to your physical traits, personality and spirit. Your soulmate and soul people will prefer *you* above all others and think that **you** are the most beautiful and gorgeous person they've ever seen – and you will also feel the same about them!! Soul connections are *highly* mutual. That is one of the reasons why they are so magical and transcendent! They are born from Love; a very high-vibrational energy and so of course they are perfect. The Universe has created love, friendships and all other relationships in such a Divine matrix of Harmony that soul people genuinely find each other their best and most perfect ideal. With soulmates of any nature – soul lovers, soul friends, soul clients, soul colleagues, etc. the fit is always mutual and perfect and the feelings are peak, extraordinary and magical!

~.Creating Your Dream Beauty/Body.~

If you do want to manifest your 'dream body' for the fun of it, I would advise to first connect with yourself and deeply appreciate your inner qualities (like we discussed in the opening paragraphs of this chapter). This makes it easier to visualize how you ideally want to look, because your physical body is a form of creative self-expression that reflects the inner you! When you are you at your best and know who you are *inside,* it tends to be expressed on the outside as the highest expression of your unique beauty – one that you probably didn't even know existed!!

As you feel great about who you are and ground yourself in your own unique inner beauty, you can begin to visualize how it would feel if you absolutely looked and felt your best. I would advise to feel feelings of delight, pride, fun, joy and passion as you see yourself in your mind's eye! These are all the qualities you'd feel if you were at your highest expression of you physically.

The physical body, in terms of sexuality and outer expression, is linked to the sacral chakra. The sacral chakra also links to life purpose and creativity! As you connect to your own purpose and express your unique creativity, it's easier to feel good and dazzlingly beautiful exactly as you are. The sacral chakra is also linked to passion, joy, fun, play, light-heartedness and unique self-expression.

As you appreciate who you are on the inside and emit

Paradise Is a State of Mind

to the universe the feeling of how you want to be (you at your best), you activate vibrations out there in the cosmos that do match what you want. You will attract circumstances, people, places and events that mirror the *feelings* of your own ideal vision back to you! You will feel amazingly fun, attractive and wonderful!! You will feel amazing about yourself and love how you look and feel, and you will attract people who deeply appreciate you and love your unique beauty inside and out! When you feel like this about yourself and love who you are, you will also feel closer to Source, and be so full of love for yourself and Life (the Universe), that you won't honestly care if people 'see' you or not! It may seem unlikely if you have yet to experience it, but as you do, you will quickly come to realize that when you feel this way about yourself and Life, nobody else's opinions are important. You have yourself and Source, and you already know how amazingly beautiful you are on the inside and out!! There is no better feeling than self-confidence on this (material) plane. There are a lot of esoteric feelings that slightly top it or maybe match it – Oneness, Love, Paradise and Gratitude, but I think they are on a very similar wavelength – when you are on the frequency of Paradise, it attracts loving yourself anyway.

-SACRAL BEAUTY-

~•BEAUTY AFFIRMATIONS•~

- I am completely powerful in my body.

- I feel very powerful in my body!

- I am exactly how I want to be.

- I am my own ideal!

- I am dazzlingly, stunningly, incredibly mind-blowingly beautiful/ good-looking/handsome.

- I am stunningly, mesmerizingly beautiful.

- I am out of this world.

- There is no-one like me.

- I love myself!!

- I am the highest, fullest, most dazzling version of me.

Paradise Is a State of Mind

- I am Divine.

- I am divine, breathtaking beauty and Love.

- I love and adore myself.

- There is no-one I'd rather be.

- I am incredible.

- I am amazing!

- I love and appreciate my unique, dazzling, individual one-of-a-kind beauty. I fully embrace and rejoice in all my special qualities and attributes.

- There is nobody quite like me.

- I am so proud of myself.

- I love and admire myself.

- I love and am delighted for myself!

- In my eyes, I am the most beautiful person in the universe.

- I am the centre of my universe.

- I am my own idol/hero.

-SACRAL BEAUTY-

- I am stunningly, hauntingly beautiful.

- I am supernaturally beyond stunning, beautiful and mindblowing.

- I am divinely gorgeous/handsome/beautiful and breathtakingly beautiful.

- People love and appreciate me.

- I love *myself*. Every day I just become more and more out of this world handsome/beautiful/good-looking and supernaturally attractive.

- I am dazzlingly, uniquely gorgeous.

- I love taking photos! My photos come out amazing and stunningly gorgeous. I look like a model, but much, much better.

- Taking photos and videos is so fun! I love and enjoy taking photos.

- I feel fully grounded and deeply happy with who I am.

- I am one with Source Energy.

Paradise Is a State of Mind

- I allow Source Energy to move through me; beautifying me, cleansing me, healing me, purifying me, and allowing my True Self to shine!!!

- The beauty of my inner Self is so rich, deep, magnetic and overwhelmingly beautiful.

- My heart is authentic, vulnerable, pure and open.

- I attract all good things into my life.

- I am a magnet for the most loving people who I love and adore!

- I only give out love and I receive love everywhere I go.

- I love life, and Life loves me!!

- There is no-one quite like me. I am my own ideal.

- I am my own perfection.

- Every day in the eternity of Life, I just become more and more radiantly, exquisitely beautiful, more and more powerfully magnetic and more and more dazzlingly gorgeous on the inside and out.

-SACRAL BEAUTY-

Every day I just become more and more one with Life. I am at home in the universe.

Paradise Is a State of Mind

11.

-EASE, FUN, BLISS, MAGIC & THE FLOW-

I read an amazing book once called *Choosing Easy World* by Julia Rogers Hamrick. This book changed my life, and this chapter is dedicated to that book.

Choosing Easy World is based on the premise that life is meant to be fun, easy, blissful and flowing, and that when we relax into the Flow, everything works out for our Highest Good effortlessly and seamlessly. Julia Rogers Hamrick writes that there is a divine 'Design for Harmony', meaning that when you tap into the feelings of flow, bliss and relaxing into a Higher Power taking care of you, handling things better than you ever could, then you access this Divine matrix for Bliss! In my experience this is so true. When you tap into high vibrations of love, bliss, joy, fun and ease, life works out

147

-EASE, FUN, BLISS, MAGIC & THE FLOW-

magically, things come to you that you were asking for
for *so* long and, during sad times when you can't access
higher-vibrational feelings of Love and magic, then
trusting the flow of life and relaxing will also get you
into the Divine matrix for Harmony!!

Julia Rogers Hamrick says: 'Easy World is the world
that Love creates.' In late 2014, I discovered author
Louise Hay, who changed my life! With the
transcendent books and affirmations of Louise Hay, I
created a living Heaven on Earth around me. After that
first year in Paradise, I stumbled across my first major
transition (from current good to Higher Good,
although I didn't see it that way at the time!), and that
was when *Choosing Easy World* magically popped into my
life!

At this time, in January 2016, I was struggling with
anxiety about moving to Barcelona, as I didn't know
anyone there, didn't have any work lined up and I was
also deeply hurt and heartbroken as had just undergone
an upsetting breakup! My intuition was leading me to
going to Barcelona. Despite this, I was still so anxious
about moving, that when I met up with two old college
friends one of them said: 'Why don't you just go there
for a holiday for two weeks, then come back and

Paradise Is a State of Mind

pretend to everyone that you couldn't find a job?' Her advice changed everything that day! Most of my anxiety virtually disappeared, and I went to Barcelona feeling relaxed, because in the back of my head I had now planned to just go on holiday, and return after two weeks like my friend suggested, pretending that I couldn't find a job! What I didn't expect, was that as soon as I set foot in Barcelona that first night, that everything would be so *easy*!! It truly was like stepping into an alternative, magical reality! I had been to Barcelona before, to trial out moving there in Summer 2014, and apart from my last day that time, I had hated it! I had stayed in the Eixample district, and for me it was so busy and soulless, and I felt alone. On my last day there, I had met two amazing Australians called Tom and Miffy, who had left me with a strong heart feeling and good memories! Nonetheless, I had still left the city feeling turned off and unenthusiastic about moving there. In spite of this, two years later, I just knew that it was my next step in life and that I had to try going there again! When I got into the taxi to go to my hostel, it took my breath away how magical and beautiful everything was! The air felt different – serene. It literally felt like a different universe, and it had nothing to do with the weather; I was going back in the

149

-EASE, FUN, BLISS, MAGIC & THE FLOW-

middle of winter! When I got to the hostel, somehow I had managed to pick the best, nicest, most FUN hostel in the middle of Barcelona (Sant Jordi Gracia), in the best district. Everything felt *so* different and everybody I met was so nice. I spent two weeks vacationing and relaxing, and in the end I actually decided to look for a job and stay after all, as I fell in love with the city from pretty much my first night back.

During the first week back in Barcelona, it struck me as bizarre that everything was somehow so easy, and so I impulsively did a Kindle book search for 'easy life'! This is where I found Julia Rogers Hamrick's *Easy World* books, and read them within a few days. They verbalized and solidified everything that I was experiencing in Barcelona, plus reading her work and being in the energy of her books (and implementing her methods) allowed me to **stay** in what I now call Easy World. These books proved to me that what I was experiencing that winter was real, and that I wasn't just imagining it! Often this does happen; you begin to experience an idea or a thought of a better way that life may be, and then shortly after, you will come across the perfect book that verbalizes and confirms everything you have been thinking! This phenomenon gives solid

Paradise Is a State of Mind

form to what you were precognizing, and gives you proof that it isn't all just in your head – because someone else has also had those same ideas, and knew it/believed in it so much that they wrote a book about it!!

I did not feel any urge to look for work or make any job applications until my last two days in Barcelona. I had prescheduled a return flight to my country shortly before coming out, for monetary reasons in case I couldn't find a job before the two weeks was up, and it was highly illogical that I wasn't feeling any urge to look for work!! However, I was practising Easy World, and following my intuition. During the final week of the trip, a scholarship opportunity popped up, to do a yoga course in Ibiza that summer, which I applied for – and got! I had always wanted to be a yoga teacher by the age of twenty-eight (I'm not sure why that age; probably precognition) and I completed my advanced yoga teacher training and had amazing clients by my twenty-eighth birthday! During my final two days of the Barcelona trip, I felt a sudden urge to browse a specific job website, and amongst the top few listings there was a job advert for a job in a nightclub that I used to script about, but didn't think existed – especially for a foreigner!! I applied for it, interviewed

151

-EASE, FUN, BLISS, MAGIC & THE FLOW-

on my penultimate day and got the job; allowing me to stay in the city for six months before the yoga course in Ibiza and completing two other career dreams I had scripted but seemed impossible!

During these months I was still in deep pain about the guy who I had broken up with before moving to Barcelona. I was deeply disappointed that it didn't work out, because before I met him, I had requested (to the Universe) that I could meet a sweet, shy foreign guy, who treated me nicely and with whom I would stay with for a minimum of one and a half years! I wasn't wanting to meet my ultimate soulmate at that point in time, as I was still very young and just wanted a nice boyfriend, in order to reset some of the not great experiences from the years before!! I got exactly what I asked for and better – my new boyfriend was Italian and I learnt a lot (culture and language) but I was confused, as when he broke up with me after just four months, I thought that we still had a year and two months to go! I accepted the situation, and asked the Universe that from that point on, that I could meet someone new by the end of the spring who would take my pain away from this breakup, and heal that wound. In early March, I ran into my old boyfriend who had broken up with me (the Italian one, the one I was upset

Paradise Is a State of Mind

about) in the middle of my neighbourhood by 'chance'! We had had no contact after breaking up, and he was blocked on my social media, so neither of us knew that the other was moving to Barcelona. I don't think he cared that much at that point where I was going anyway! It turned out that he'd been living three doors down from me the entire time, in Barcelona, in the exact same neighbourhood on the street adjacent to my hostel! He too had had the same idea to move to Barcelona, around the same time as me. We took it as a sign to get back together, and as we both knew that we weren't the other's 'One' (ultimate soulmate), we stayed together but in a more casual, relaxed way for another fourteen months. It mutually benefited both of us, as we had a great time together, and this time, because I had had time to naturally get bored of him/fall out of love, the second and final breakup was *completely* painless!! He had just moved from his space in my heart from lover to friend over those final fourteen months. It was truly magic! That is the power and magic of Easy World! I spent the entire year and a half of the next year (2016-mid 2017) in Easy World, first in Barcelona, and then in Ibiza with my yoga teacher! It truly was magical: a different, High-Vibrational reality, where everything does indeed work

-EASE, FUN, BLISS, MAGIC & THE FLOW-

out in awe-inspiring, jaw-dropping, unbelievable ways! There were points interspersed within these times where it did look like things weren't going to work out, but in the end they always somehow magically did. The way things come together and Flow in Easy World is truly extraordinary and out of this world!

It really is true that 'Easy World is the reality that Love creates.' When you tap into the feelings of love, joy, gratitude, bliss, ease, fun and flow regularly, as much as you can, your whole life does indeed become Magic, and a living Paradise! You truly can create Heaven on Earth – and it is just as real and valid as what Rogers Hamrick calls the 'Difficult World' matrix. Difficult World is just the normal, boring, difficult strugglesome life we have all experienced: a life without spirituality, Positivity and Love!! Tuesday May Thomas, in her book *The Law of Vibration*, says that 'the world' is a place where we reside in when we are living from the mind and not the heart. 'The Earth' is where we reside when we experience vibrations of Love and Good from our own heart; projecting them out into our world, which then becomes Heaven on Earth. Heaven on Earth is the world you create around you when you live from your heart. The heart – Love – is so Powerful that it

Paradise Is a State of Mind

magically transforms the most difficult circumstances, and creates your own living Heaven on Earth around you.

I used to think that worrying would keep me safe and protect me. I had anxiety for a long time; basically lifelong, because deep down, I was afraid to let it go! I believed deep down that if I just worried about something for long enough, trying to figure out a solution, that I'd resolve it! My life was basically one problem after the other, and although I did have bouts of joy, life was mainly overshadowed by anxiety, worry and problem-solving. I think when you spend your life dwelling on and worrying about problems, you end up creating a life of problems, where there is always another problem to solve. **Worrying doesn't actually resolve problems; high vibrations do!** When you finally let go of a problem; giving up on it or even stopping caring, that is when the problem magically works itself out!!

It isn't always about letting go. A lot of the time, just getting into a very high vibration (Love vibration) will also rearrange reality around you, as the Positive energy is *so* strong, that the agony of the problem is incompatible with Love!! I experienced this for about a

-EASE, FUN, BLISS, MAGIC & THE FLOW-

year before I read *Choosing Easy World*, and things fell into place when Rogers Hamrick described the phenomenon also in her book. This confirmed it to me – that when you get into a very high vibration, problems cannot exist at that higher frequency, and so they spontaneously and magically resolve themselves!

It is also worth noting that the energies of fun, ease, joy, relaxation and peaceful non-attachment will manifest things far quicker, and at a much higher vibration, than trying to do things the hard way. The hard way really is unnecessary!! We have been brought up in 'the real world' where struggle, suffering and 'hustle' is taught as mandatory!! In Difficult World, struggle and hustle is something to be proud of, and 'the harder you work, the luckier you get!' I worked this way for many years, and ultimately I found that when you work hard, suffer and struggle, the outcome tends to be unfulfilling and disappointing. It also tends to be temporary, meaning that what does manifest will disappear quickly, or not stick around.

When you take the easy path, relaxing into ease, Flow, joy and Trust, and following the path of joy or least resistance, that is when the perfect things you need magically show up, and your results are deeply

Paradise Is a State of Mind

fulfilling, joyful and Love-filled! Love-filled results last a very long time, and tend to be permanent or very durable. When Love-filled things do end, they do so harmoniously, and at the end of a very natural conclusion!! Of course, there will be times (like in Chapter 7) when no fun, easy or joyful option seems to be available!! In these times, the path of Flow is just to pick the best available path; the option with the least resistance, that feels the easiest, most relaxed, joyful and flowing compared to all the others!! Or the best of a bad bunch. Following that path will still connect you to Grace, Ease, Joy, Flow and Magic!!

I think that if you are still reading this book, then you have probably already experienced what I am describing here in your own life. This chapter is just confirming to you and solidifying everything you have already experienced in your own world. The Universe is showing you it is definitely real, because other people have experienced it as well, and wrote books about it! We are all connected. The Universe is confirming to us that we are correct in our experiences, and we are not alone in our journeys! We have all the resources and unseen invisible guides and friends that will appear at the divine right time to support us!!

~•EASE, MAGIC & THE FLOW

AFFIRMATIONS•~

- Life is easy!

- Life is so *incredibly* fun and easy!

- Everything is so easy and magical!

- Life is a Wonder. Everywhere I go, I see magic and miracles surround me! Life loves me.

- I live in a reality of Bliss and Flow.

- I live in a world of magic and miracles.

- I live in a universe of wonder and bliss.

Paradise Is a State of Mind

- I live in a world of incredible wonder.

- I am in awe every day of the magic and miracles that unfold around me!!

- I am always wonderfully divinely protected!! I live in a cocoon of Magic and Divine Wonder.

- I live in a world of Bliss and Miracles.

- Every day is fun, exciting and a unique experience for me. Every day is filled with wonder and magic.

- My gratitude and love creates a world of bliss and wonder! I give out awe and gratitude, and I receive back Paradise and Love in return.

- The more grateful I am, the more I receive to be grateful and in awe about!

- Gratitude, love and wonder are the greatest gifts I can give to the Universe. I create my mind full of beautiful and grateful thoughts, and my loving heart and mind manifest Paradise and Heaven on Earth all around me.

-EASE, FUN, BLISS, MAGIC & THE FLOW-

- I relax in the Flow of Life. Everything is so beautifully, wondrously and lovingly taken care of around me!

- Life unfolds before me and around me, in the most magical, exciting blissful ways.

- I live in a cocoon of Bliss and Miracles.

- Love surrounds me wherever I go. I live in a universe full of Love.

- I relax and flow with life. I am always magically taken care of, supported, provided for and loved in the most fulfilling, exciting, extravagant joyous ways!

- Life loves to impress me. I am the love of the Universe's heart.

- I relax joyously in the Flow. Life constantly carries me to the best, most magical, most miraculous and exciting experiences. I love and trust Life.

Paradise Is a State of Mind

- Life loves me! I am always receiving incredible gifts. I am constantly brought together with and saturated in the most joyful satisfying experiences! Life loves me, and I am deeply fulfilled.

- I accept the incredible deep love and care the Universe has for me.   My well-being and happiness are the Universe's pride and joy.

- I love Life! Life *always* takes care of me. Life loves me. I am worthy of the very best that Life has to offer, and the Universe loves to gift me with its extraordinary surprises and treasures!!!

- I live in a universe filled with Love. Love surrounds me everywhere I go. Love dwells within me, flows through me and radiates out to the entire world. I live in an ocean of Love.

- I love life! Everything is blissful, flowing, easy, FUN and magical!! I live in a cocoon of awe, bliss and extravagant wonder.

-EASE, FUN, BLISS, MAGIC & THE FLOW-

12.

-PARADISE, LOVE, GRATITUDE AND HEAVEN ON EARTH-

L ove truly is the answer.

I believe that Love, Joy, Gratitude, Fun and Peace are the important priorities in creating our own personal living Paradise, a life that is pure Heaven on Earth. When you put out Joy, Gratitude, Love, Bliss and Fun into the universe, life brings back to you people, places, circumstances and events that mirror the vibrations of those energies. Really, what we want is to feel bliss, love and Paradise as much as possible. When you feel Paradise, nothing else is needed.

When you live a life filled with love, Oneness and joy, you understand that inner fulfilment and love are the only things that really matter in this life! You could be a billionaire, rich, successful and famous with a perfect body and married to the best person on Earth, and still be unhappy! Likewise, you can be just starting out on your journey, with only the confidence that your dreams and desires will inevitably manifest, no evidence in sight, and still be filled with Love, Paradise and Bliss. Ironically, love, joy and gratitude feelings manifest your dreams and desires by themselves anyway even if you didn't ask or expect them to – or even believe it possible!!

Another reason why love, joy and gratitude are top priorities is because when you do make your dreams happen or the Universe manifests them, if you lack love and gratitude on the inside then what manifests is ultimately disappointing. However, if you learn to love, cultivate and enjoy feelings of bliss and joy now, in the present moment, you will attract them back to you in future tenfold. Tending to your present moment now insures your future.

Love is so powerful that armed with Love, you don't even need anything else! Love is such a powerful, intelligent Energy that already knows what you want and delights in bringing that together for the Highest

Paradise Is a State of Mind

Good of all. Love is benevolent, kind and will lead you to your Higher Good. Love is God, and God knows the desires of your heart so will ensure they happen.

Love opens all doors, even ones that seemed to be sealed shut or non-existent! Love smooths out and magically resolves all problems. Love brings all your desires made manifest in the easiest, most beautiful miraculous ways – even desires you'd forgotten about or no longer thought possible! And yet there is so much more to Love than just getting what you want.

Love also heightens your intuition so it is razor-sharp. Love awakens your heart which vibrates at the higher planes, awakening your psychic abilities and telepathy. You will often experience heightened and awakened psychic powers when you open your heart. Telepathy and coincidences with people – namely the people closest to you – will increase, and you may even share dreams with loved ones, or experience precognition. These are just a few examples of the powers of Love.

Love is the number one key to Paradise. The Universe is made of Love, and so are you. It is Love and so are you! How wonderful. When you relax into Love, which is your true nature, the Universe rejoices

-PARADISE, LOVE, GRATITUDE AND HEAVEN ON EARTH-

because you are in a pure state of Being, and Being attracts more of itself – at its essence, pure Potentiality: Love, Joy and Paradise.

I believe the second joint number one key to Paradise is gratitude. Gratitude is a potent form of Love; when you are grateful you are acknowledging the good in life and seeing God everywhere. God is Love and Good. Gratitude also creates the purest vibration of fulfilment. Gratitude and Love together are Heaven on Earth. Gratitude says, 'I am always receiving. There is so much good in my life! I already have everything I want and need.' Gratitude forces you to dwell on all the good in life and what you have, and ultimately gives you the real awareness of a benevolent Higher Power loving and blessing you. When your mind constantly dwells on what you have and how lucky you are, you become a magnet for more Love, Good and Paradise. Everything you're searching for is within you.

Sometimes we look for fulfilment on the outside, chasing goals! Goals are thrilling and exciting and we desire them for a reason; because our souls want fulfilment and expansion and to create! However, if you have goals but don't already carry inner fulfilment, love and gratitude within, often when you achieve the

Paradise Is a State of Mind

goal it will be disappointing and unfulfilling/not what you expected. However, if you already cultivate emotions of gratitude, joy and love inside you at the centre of You, you colour this vibration into the world everywhere you go, forming and shaping your reality with gratitude, love and joy – pure Paradise. These highest-vibrational energies come back to you mirrored all around as a world of infinite Light, Love, joy, fun, passion, bliss, Creation, freedom and Oneness.

If you ever don't know what to do, feel lost or helpless, then concentrate on Love! Love is a form of Quantum Intelligence – it already knows everything and what is good for you. Love sorts out all your problems and brings you what you need that makes you feel even more Love and gratitude. When things manifest and you are already in a loving space, what manifests will be deeply satisfying, exceed expectations, be better than your wildest dreams and come with extras you didn't even know you wanted!! Life is so good, benevolent and loving. It is an intelligent, alive Force that created us and made itself one with us. Love is inside us all the time and we *are* Love. You are never alone because you have Love inside you all the time. Rumi, the famous Sufi poet, said: Never feel alone

167

-PARADISE, LOVE, GRATITUDE AND HEAVEN ON EARTH-

because you have the entire Universe inside you. You are one with the Higher Power, the One who created the universe and created you, and it is with you everywhere and at all times. Even when it doesn't look like it is, it is there working diligently and lovingly and tirelessly behind the scenes, making sure a dark period turns out to be rich soil for the most gorgeous blossomings! Life really is amazing.

To create Paradise, think thoughts of Paradise. Paradise is Oneness, the Present moment, Joy, Awe, Wonder, Bliss, Fun, Love and deep Appreciation. Paradise is when you walk past the most beautiful flowers in the spring and the awe and breathtaken feeling you feel when you watch a stunning sunrise. Love and Awe are when you step outside at night and feel the Universe around you, surrounding you as you look up to an inky night sky strewn with thousands of beautiful, cold, distant, twinkling stars. The stars are always there for you. The Moon and Sun are always there for you. The Universe is all around us, and connecting and immersing yourself in nature is one of the fastest shortcuts to experiencing the awe and wonder and sheer joy of Presence. There are so many countless things in nature to fill you with a sense of awe, joy and Oneness: the bees buzzing gently going

Paradise Is a State of Mind

from flower to flower collecting their nectar, the colourful sights of fresh spring blooms and the fragrance of jasmine on a hot summer's night. Feeling warm sand on your body and immersing yourself in a cool ocean in the summer is one of the most joyful things you can experience!! Looking up at vivid blue skies, especially if there are outlines of tree branches, birds, or flowers against them... fluffy, white cumulus clouds add an extra adornment. Hearing the sweet, pure sounds of a singing robin, blackbird or any songbird's voice can instantly transport you to Paradise. I believe birdsong vibrates at the frequency of Heaven on Earth, and we are surrounded by it.

Nature is full of Love; it is especially evident in the spring and summer, when all the animals are excitedly preparing to have babies and then fiercely caring for these babies. From a low vibration, where perception is more negative, it appears to be survival instinct. From the higher vibrations and standpoint of Love, you see the truth of what is really going on – pure Love. The animals meet, have children and raise them out of pure Love; Nature hardwires them to fall in love with each other and their children because Nature *is* Love. Like in our own lives, Love is ever-present, and in the

-PARADISE, LOVE, GRATITUDE AND HEAVEN ON EARTH-

winter it is still at work underneath the soil. There are tree seeds like chestnuts that won't germinate without first being buried in cold, dark soils. They need these harsh conditions to grow and flourish! Even when it appears like nothing is happening, new life, growth and tremendous progress are always happening beneath the surface.

Paradise is Love, bliss and Oneness and you can create a living Paradise for yourself when you make it the number one priority. Other daily priorities aren't as important as creating Love inside you, because when you concentrate on a to-do list or getting things done (that you're only doing to get to where you want to be) then that focus creates more of endless 'things to do.' When you are already vibrating fulfilment and Paradise, anything that needs to be done to reach your desires will be effortless, fun, easy, joyous and obvious, and will not feel like work at all! Paradise really is the answer.

When you vibrate Paradise, Love and fulfilment, these vibrations are so powerful that they crowd out any negative and lower vibrations from your mind and your life. When your life and your mind fill with the thoughts, feelings and vibrations of Paradise, there is

Paradise Is a State of Mind

little room for anything else. Paradise solves all problems and makes answers to decisions obvious, so there is no need to put Paradise on hold in order to worry to solve a problem! Worrying is a very weak, not very powerful and low-vibrational energy. I believe that it can't manifest the worst to happen – rather it just creates more to be worried about! This endless cycle repeats on loop, lowering your quality of life. Your quality of life is directly dependent on the thoughts and feelings you are experiencing on a regular basis. It is that simple. When you vibrate Love, Paradise and fulfilment on a regular basis, you feel happier, you vibrate higher and more joyful, blissful frequencies out into the universe, and more of that same Prima Materia Energy is brought back to you in form.

There are many ways to feel bliss and Paradise, and they are different for everyone! Listening to music you love, being with and appreciating nature, going to a party, being with friends, doing what you love and what sets your soul on fire, reading an uplifting book, practising positive affirmations or doing something really fun are some examples. The activity itself isn't important; it's how it makes you *feel.* If you do activities

-PARADISE, LOVE, GRATITUDE AND HEAVEN ON EARTH-

(including reading spiritual books, doing affirmations, scripting, or visualizing, etc.) that make you feel joyful, high-vibrational, filled with love or fulfilled, keep doing them as often as you can! The more you do them, the more you are practising and neurologically rewiring to become the vibration of Paradise.

The more you practise, the easier it'll get and Paradise will pull itself towards you. You can have a bad day or a bad mood or something goes wrong, and because Heaven is so strong, it may take a few hours, days or even weeks but something will happen to pick back up again and bring you back to Paradise. It is fine to have these lulls and bad days because allowing yourself to feel your emotions, embracing them and being sad allows the Universe to hold you and be there for you, flowing all around you! It also contributes to the Flow. I believe these sad moments are the pure beauty and part of the colours of Life. We were given all the emotions to experience, and when we feel sadness and allow ourselves to be held – experiencing what is a natural feeling – we allow the Flow of the Universe. The Good always outweighs the sad periods in the end anyway, so it is necessary and good to allow yourself to just *feel*.

Paradise Is a State of Mind

When you are in the Love vibration, and you are truly happy, you also tend to have less thoughts. When you are channelling pure Joy, Love, happiness, fun and bliss through your being, you generally tend to not think; just feel. Feelings are the epitome of life! When you are bathing in the glow and high transcendent energy of pure Life Force, it makes sense that you would feel more. Overthinking is what happens when we sink into the lower vibrations. When you are practised immersing yourself in the vibrations of love, gratitude, joy and all the other highest-currency feelings, you will find yourself thinking less and less!! It truly is blissful. You will be more in your body, more in the Present moment, more in your heart and more in your soul. Your intuition will be clear because your intuition resides in your body and your heart, rather than the mind.

Practise Paradise, become Paradise and Love vibrationally and you will become Paradise; you will become a magnet for all Good, Love and the highest, most fulfilling, loving and beautiful experiences, people and existences in the universe!

The potential for love, Good and Paradise is unlimited. Love is creative and expansive, the Universe is Love and

-PARADISE, LOVE, GRATITUDE AND HEAVEN ON EARTH-

as the Universe is expansive and infinite, Love is the same. The energy of Love only increases the more you feel it. It is a limitless, ever-expanding and ever-creative energy. Love opens all doors and when you walk through these doors, into love, joy and all good, you only experience more of the same. I used to procrastinate on doing things that got me into the Love feeling because I was scared it would run out, so I wanted to save it! What I realized after time was that when you move into Love, Love attracts more of itself and expands; it never runs out. You may read a book, listen to music, meet someone who makes you feel love and think that they are the source, so you have to be careful with them or not overdo it. The truth is that there is always more Love, and the best way to create a life full of infinite Love is to move into Love now, and watch with delight and enjoy as it unfolds into more Love. Don't procrastinate Paradise because the more Paradise you are, the more you attract and the more you attract, the more it creates and expands. Love and Paradise are infinite, never run out, only ever create more of themselves and are never-ending.

-EPILOGUE-

There is no end to the Paradise you can create. Your ability to create good in your life is limitless. Love and Paradise have no limits. Love is infinite and endless. Love multiplies and the more Love you give out, the more you get back. Love multiplies, shares and has no boundaries. The Universe is infinitely expanding and with it, our capacity to Love the same!

Being positive doesn't mean we are perfect. There is no such thing! Perfection is void of creativity, colour or expansion. As humans we are made imperfect and paradoxically we are perfect to the Universe that way! Within imperfection lies room for learning, growth, expansion, creativity and authenticity. We are loved by the Universe *exactly* as we are. This includes our bad days and sad periods.

-EPILOGUE-

When I first started on my Paradise journey in late 2014, I was starting with anxiety and depression that had been pretty much lifelong. I was feeling nostalgic for that time in 2014-2015; the very beginning of the journey, thinking how perfect it had all been and how blissful I had been 24/7 in discovering and living Paradise! Well, when I looked through my Kindle order history at the beginning of writing this book in early 2023, I received a pleasant shock! It transpired that I had still had days or even weeks where I'd felt anxious and/or depressed during those paradisiacal times; I had just forgotten about them! I also met recently with a dear friend who I had attracted from the Paradise frequency in 2015. He reminded me of how deeply loved and accepted I was back in 2015 even though at that time, I'd still had low moods and bad days! The friends, employers, colleagues, neighbours, customers, boyfriend and everyone else in my life who had come in at that time on that frequency had loved me deeply even though I was not perfect. In fact, I think when I had my sad days, cried or even had brief moments of childishness it actually made us closer! I never experienced as much love as I did in 2015 so I can't help but think there is a correlation. I have noticed that the times when I feel closest to the

Paradise Is a State of Mind

Universe are not only the happiest and most blissful moments in my life, but also the times where I'm deeply sad or heartbroken, and the Universe makes its presence known with a miracle; small or big but obviously of Divine intervention. It is these times that mean just as much as the blissful miraculous times, because at the heart of Paradise is Oneness. In addition, the one friend I have had who I have loved and admired the most in my life so far once told me one night: 'It is okay to cry. I cried last night about [her previous employer], about [the guy she liked a lot at the time who'd let her down]. About everything' and I still remember the chills I felt down my spine because her beauty was even more luminous and radiant in her sadness. It is these vulnerable moments of authenticity that bring us closer to one another. It is a wonderful feeling to know that the ones you love, and who also love you, love and accept you exactly as you are. Knowing that the people you love are there for you and being supported during the worst or most challenging times is a priceless and incomparable blessing. True, real love is supportive and unconditional.

As you are positive and loving as much as you can be, the Universe rewards your efforts and brings your love and positive energy back to you tenfold. It doesn't

-EPILOGUE-

matter if you slip up and have days where you feel terrible and disconnected. We are always doing our best we can, at any given time with what we have. The Universe knows we are only human so of course we will have bad days. On these low days, I think the best thing you can do is not necessarily force yourself to think positive thoughts, rather just to soothe yourself and allow yourself to relax and do anything that makes you feel better. Often that is nothing 'spiritual' and something comforting like watching your favourite TV show, having your favourite hot drink or snack or chatting with a friend. When you follow the flow this way, after time your vibration naturally raises back up and you will feel more aligned and connected to the Flow, eventually ready to access those high points again. Life is very forgiving, gentle and nurturing. It is still working on your manifestations even when you're having a bad day. Allow life to be there for you, do your best and know your best is enough!!

We also don't need to know everything. We do our part to be positive and send out our positivity into the universe, to vibrate Love, Gratitude and Heaven, but there is always a greater Mystery and Intelligence to life. I believe we are not meant to know everything. We are as positive and as loving as we can be,

Paradise Is a State of Mind

appreciating life with gratitude, joy and optimism and knowing that all and only good things are coming to us! Simultaneously, we let go of the need to control life because we know that there is a much grander Intelligence in the universe that knows how to fulfil us in ways far beyond our limited human imagination. This is something to be grateful for. Within the passivity of the uncertain and the unknown lies blissful innocence, gratitude, humility, openness, curiosity, adventure and excitement! Let life surprise you!

If you enjoyed this book, I also have another shorter book called *Positive Affirmations: Positivity, Luck, Success, Receiving & Dreams.* You may also like to check out the work of the main people who influenced me so far in writing this book and on my journey. These people are what I call 'Heaven on Earth teachers'! They are the teachers I go back to time after time; the ones who taught me what it was like to feel and *be* Paradise and to create Heaven on Earth all around you. You can find them in the 'Acknowledgements' chapter at the end of this book.

Thank you for reading. I hope it helped you in some way!

180

Paradise Is a State of Mind

-ACKNOWLEDGEMENTS-

I will be ever-grateful to the following people, who signposted me the way on feeling happy and fulfilled on the inside first, and inadvertently how to manifest pure Paradise and Heaven on Earth all around! When you feel full and happy inside, what you create is Heaven all around you. I am grateful to the following teachers, without whom I may always have been chasing goals and seeking fulfilment on the outside before realizing it comes from within:

Louise Hay – Author

Louise Hay has a way of making you feel Heaven on Earth and pure Paradise. Bliss ensues whenever you read or listen to Louise Hay! She really walked her talk. The energy of a teacher is very important and that is one of the reasons why Hay's work is so powerful. It is

-ACKNOWLEDGEMENTS-

laced with potency and transcendence. Whenever I read or listen to Louise Hay, I feel optimistic and 'full,' like I already have everything I need and yet at the same time, I feel excited and positive to create all the good that is coming to my life!! Louise Hay changed my life. I can always turn to her work when I'm not feeling my best, and I am constantly finding new layers and meanings in her work! Louise Hay was also the first person who really taught me the value of simplicity. Often, the most powerful and profound changes and transformations you will go through in life are rooted in simplicity. Source energy is intuitive, uncomplicated and clear.

Claire Winchester – Hypnotherapist –
https://clairewinchester.co.uk/

I have been working with Claire Winchester since late 2014, and she is the one person who set me off on my spiritual journey! I was at the worst point in my life when I met Claire. As fate or Divine intervention would have it, my usual therapist (who was also very good), was off sick that day and so I was introduced to Claire. I realized looking back that that encounter was

Paradise Is a State of Mind

meant to be, as I couldn't progress in the direction my life was meant to go with my old therapist – whereas Claire opened the door wide open for me!! What Claire teaches is perfectly compatible with Chapter 7 and also Chapter 1 of this book. Claire introduced me to the idea of positive thinking, gratitude, that positivity is a choice and that we can all choose to empower ourselves by choosing to think positive. She also taught me to *be* a better person by introducing me to gratitude, looking at how situations can be *for* you and help you to grow and also to see all the good and magic in life!!

Miranda Kerr – Author

Miranda Kerr was also one of the people whose work truly changed my life! Along with Claire Winchester and Louise Hay, Miranda Kerr's book *Treasure Yourself* changed my world, and was how I ended up finding real happiness and creating a life I loved. The day I got back to my town from my first ever session with Claire Winchester, Kerr's book was on display in the front window of my local Waterstones! At that time, I was very young and loved fashion. Life knew that by using

-ACKNOWLEDGEMENTS-

these channels, it would catch my attention! I bought the book because it was by Kerr, and the synchronicity and Divine intervention behind this when I began reading blew me away!! Together with Claire Winchester, Kerr's book taught me to be more grateful, loving, positive, appreciative and resilient, and *Treasure Yourself* led me to Louise Hay.

Charlotta Hughes – Life Coach –
https://www.charlottahughes.com/

I have been working with life coach Charlotta Hughes since Autumn 2014 and she is the best coach. I found her after googling 'life coaching', and she came up as the winner of best life coach award in my country (the UK)! After speaking to her on the phone, I booked my first package and began working with her; it was soon not hard to understand why she had won the award!

I often looked back on Charlotta as 'magic glue' in reverse – meaning that whenever I was particularly stuck in a situation, a few days, weeks or even months after I'd worked with her, the situation I was in would become 'unstuck' by itself and life flowed towards the

Paradise Is a State of Mind

direction I wanted! It was like magic. This is the power of a really good coach! Charlotta helped me to tap into my intuition, gain clarity and look at things in ways I'd never considered before that were infinitely more helpful and freeing than the way I'd been looking at them! They were also more balanced and realistic. She is very compassionate and non-judgemental.

Working with my coach always helps me to feel more empowered, confident, worthy and deserving of and able to achieve my goals! The vast majority of top athletes, high performers, business leaders, etc. all have coaches. I constantly have new insights and breakthroughs when I work with Charlotta.

Julia Rogers Hamrick – Author

Julia Rogers Hamrick wrote the Easy World series and remains to this day one of the most powerful and major influences in my life! Her *Easy World* books are not presently super well-known but her frequency, energy, knowledge and wisdom are far beyond most popular spiritual teachers today. Her teachings state that love, joy, ease and high vibrations are the only thing we need and that life is meant to be easy!! They are also based

-ACKNOWLEDGEMENTS-

on the Love, Intelligence and Wisdom of a Higher Power. Julia Rogers Hamrick teaches from a place of deep wisdom and personal experience, and you can feel the loving and transcendent energy coming through the pages.

~.Soul Journey.~

I believe that ultimately, your soul is the Master Teacher for your life and leads you to the perfect resources at the right time in your life.

I subscribe to the theory that our soul has set up a curriculum of lessons and guidance for what we need to learn in order to evolve into our highest and happiest selves! Your soul is connected to the Higher Plan for your life and anchors you to the course via your intuition, and Divine intervention as and when needed. We follow our inner guidance when walking along the path. You can never steer wrong when you follow your own intuition; it is a form of divine guidance. I also believe we are being divinely guided, protected and watched over at all times. This is where Divine intervention comes in. If we are at a point in our journey where we are about to make a glaring mistake that would steer us off course, Life steps in to

~.Soul Journey.~

intervene! Something will happen to protect you from an event, or from ignoring your intuition and making an irrefutable mistake. Rest assured that if you ever feel you have made a glaring mistake, this is impossible! If the Universe actually allowed you to go ahead and make a 'glaring mistake', then it is for a reason and something good is designated to come out of it in the end. This is true even for the worst and darkest of situations. Everything happens for a reason and happens for your soul's highest growth – and happiness. Life *wants* you to be happy and fulfilled. Your highest growth and the subsequent best times often spring from the deepest destruction and life's storms. Life is loving and benevolent. Miranda Kerr says in *Treasure Yourself* that after every hard time, whether it is a challenge that turns your life upside down or a simple obstacle that gets in the way of where you want to go, there is *always* an act of creation.

I also believe that Life moves in spirals. The Universe is profoundly and unchangeably oriented towards growth, healing and Light. It is the natural course and order of Life to move towards deeper layers and levels of healing, as we constantly become our highest, happiest and healthiest selves! We are always

Paradise Is a State of Mind

becoming more and more Light and Love.

Throughout this process, we may encounter situations we really thought we'd already healed or overcome – and it can be very frustrating to find we're experiencing them again!! It is just old energy on its way out. Your reaction to it shows you how much you have really healed from it or not. If you feel angry, frustrated or very reactionary to it, then you know it isn't truly out of your system – once you are truly and genuinely over something, there is not enough energetic hook left in that pattern to get a rise out of you! Instead, you will find it funny, bizarre or even comical that the situation is even showing up again, because you *know* you are over it!! Eventually, the energy will lose so much hook and be such a non-issue for you that it will fade or spiral out of your energy field completely.

Be proud of and happy for yourself wherever you are on your journey. Remember that everything happens in Divine Timing, and **we are always doing the very best we can**. When it's time to truly transcend something, Life will help you and you will fully heal it completely. You are perfect right where you are, and you are doing *so* well.

~.Soul Journey.~

I believe life lessons are merely learning opportunities from one experience to another. The more you go through, the more you evolve and grow! Get out there, be fearless in making mistakes and learn, grow and evolve through your own process!! The more you go through, the more you grow. The most successful individuals in life fail ten times as much as people living ordinary lives, and they are not so afraid to make mistakes. We all feel fear – the difference is that successful people feel the fear and do it anyway – they don't allow doubts or fears to put them off or deter them from trying! High risk = high reward. You also really can't care what others think about you, because the vast majority of people are sheep and there is no point being influenced by their opinion. If you want to be influenced by anyone's opinion, make sure it is by the opinion of someone who is successful in the way you want to be and thinks with their own mind. You want to learn from the best if you want to be the best.

I believe life is lovingly, divinely guided by our Higher Self and so everybody's journey is individual, unique and different. What works for one person may not work for another and so this is why, really, your best teacher can always only ever be your own life experience! You can read something in a hundred

Paradise Is a State of Mind

different books, a hundred different times by a hundred different people and yet you still won't truly learn the lesson until you've gone out there and made the mistake (usually more than several times!!) yourself!! Neurologically, this is also how we learn. Actively repeating the same action and correcting ourselves from our mistakes builds up the myelin sheath around the neural circuitry in our brain, biologically conducting us to be better skilled, more efficient, faster and better geared towards performing or behaving in a way we want.

It is also normal to change mentors or move on to different teachers, lessons, books, etc. as we grow and change. Some we will return to time after time, but many we will outgrow. Life never goes backwards – only forwards and upwards. Life is inherently, divinely geared towards healing, transformation and higher levels of Love. It is normal that the same experiences or lessons won't resonate with you when you're at a further, higher point in your journey. We also don't learn 100% of what we need from any one given person or situation at a time. Life is a complex coalescence of levels, layers and parts; we accumulate wisdom from the various people we meet and combine it with our own knowledge and experiences. I believe that really what is happening when we meet the right teacher, book or resource is that we are connecting with the frequency of our own soul. The book, guide or resource is a medium and we are connecting to the essence of our own Journey and Higher Self through it. We move through points of time, but really what we are doing is accessing points where we connect with our Self. We are not designed to be carbon copies of one another. When you respect and appreciate the value and weight of your own life experiences, you gain strength, self-confidence and self-appreciation along with gratitude and recognition for others and the roles they've played along your journey.

I also think that encounters are divinely arranged. We are meant to meet certain people at certain points in our lives, and we are all led to each other so we can mutually benefit each other's higher growth at that time. Even bad experiences are all part of the process. You can learn from bad encounters and poor experiences just as much as you learn from the best, lightest, happiest and most joyous times of life!! Getting involved with the wrong people, going through a painful challenge or experiencing the negative consequences of ignoring your own intuition and making your own mistakes, greatly strengthens your

Paradise Is a State of Mind

ability to listen to and heed your own inner voice in future. It will strengthen your own inner guidance so much that you will become highly intuitive and grow in tremendous respect for yourself! In *The Luck Factor* by Richard Wiseman, Wiseman states that lucky people have an uncanny ability to listen to and act upon their intuition! According to Wiseman, this is because lucky people have subconsciously learnt from past experiences – all the business deals, shady friends or lovers and 'bad people' or events that left them bruised. Subconsciously, lucky people stored in their memory their past mistakes or bad events, and have used them to create a superstrong intuition that has an uncanny ability to now steer them away from the wrong people and situations, and towards the right ones!! When you have a strong intuition, your life moves more efficiently and quicker towards the good stuff and you are more deeply connected to your heart, and your Self.

Life ultimately is a rich, colourful and unique journey. We all walk down the path as individuals, but we are never alone on the road. There are always the perfect, Divine destined people who accompany us on the road at each perfect stage in our lives.

We absorb what we learn from one another, combine it

~.Soul Journey.~

with our own wisdom and personal experience and we are destined to develop, grow and bloom into the dazzlingly beautiful, unique and multifaceted individuals that we are!! I like to liken the spirit journey to the formation of an opal, after my mother told me the story of how these precious gemstones are formed. Opals are stunningly unique, richly-coloured and dazzling individuals and each one is different from another – however all are enchantingly beautiful and wealth with knowledge, experience and wisdom. Opals are ancient; formed from millions of years of elementary reactions with the Earth's crust. Silica deposits within water seep into cracks and voids within the Earth, which are there from natural faults and decomposing fossils. The water deposits these silica sediments inside the cracks and voids and evaporates, and the sediment eventually becomes the stunning multi-colours and specks of the rainbowed opals. We too, are designed to become our highest, wisest and most uniquely beautiful Selves through our interactions with Nature, i.e. life's challenges; the wind, the storms, the rain, thunder & lightning, the Moon and the fire. Yet there is also the good, the positivity and the Sun, the pure Love and freedom, the stars, the sky, sand, trees, flowers and fauna, etc. The joy and

Paradise Is a State of Mind

bliss of life also shape us and form us into who we are meant to be just as much as the challenges! It is all a generous amalgamation of life experiences for our Highest Growth, greatest Beauty and Potential. Opals take millions of years to form the gleaming arcane beauty we can see today. You will only ever become wiser, more powerful and more beautiful & magnetic as you move through life. Inner beauty is always translated and reflected on the outer. You never need to fear life and where it is going, because Life is always there for you and moving towards your ultimate Greatness, Beauty, Wisdom and Potential!! When you know that every experience benefits you, you can approach life with gratitude and appreciation, no matter the weather!! Within experience lies an opportunity.

~.Soul Journey.~

-RECOMMENDED READING-

I highly recommend the following books. I have read thousands of books, as I'm sure anyone who is still reading this also has! These books listed are the ones that made a difference to me, that I still re-read and that I am grateful for, for contributing to my journey:

~•Books•~

Treasure Yourself by Miranda Kerr

I Can Do It by Louise Hay

You Can Create an Exceptional Life by Cheryl Richardson & Louise Hay

-RECOMMENDED READING-

The Power Is Within You by Louise Hay

Power Thoughts by Louise Hay

Heart Thoughts by Louise Hay

Gratitude! A Way of Life by Michele Gold & Louise Hay

The Magic Path of Intuition by Florence Scovel Shinn & Louise Hay

You Can Heal Your Life by Louise Hay

Who Moved My Cheese: An Amazing Way to Deal with Change in Your Work and in Your Life by Spencer Johnson

You Can Heal Your Heart: Finding Peace After a Breakup, Divorce, or Death by David Kestrel & Louise Hay

Change Your Life In Seven Days by Paul McKenna

Just Ask the Universe: A No-Nonsense Guide to Manifesting Your Dreams by Michael Samuels

The Joy of Burnout: How the End of the World Can Be a New Beginning by Dr Dina Glouberman

Paradise Is a State of Mind

The 3 Things That Will Change Your Destiny Today! by Paul McKenna

Love Will Find You: 9 Magnets to Bring You and Your Soulmate Together by Kathryn Alice

Learned Optimism: How to Change Your Mind and Your Life by Martin E. P. Seligman

The Luck Factor: The Scientific Study of the Lucky Mind by Richard Wiseman

Choosing Easy World: A Guide to Opting Out of Struggle and Strife and Living in the Amazing Realm Where Everything Is Easy by Julia Rogers Hamrick

-RECOMMENDED READING-

ABOUT THE AUTHOR

Alexia Eden is an English author, singer and actor. She is a RYT500hr yoga teacher with YogaAlliance USA and has a BSc degree in biomedicine. She has worked in the financial services industry in London and in the hospitality, nightlife and events industries in Ibiza and Barcelona. She loves travelling, electronic music, languages, nature and animals.

Edenyogaibiza.com

Printed in Great Britain
by Amazon